D0571054

Jane Austen Cover to Cover

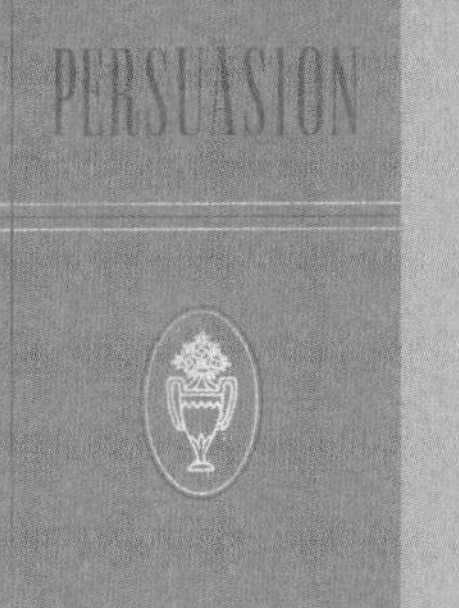

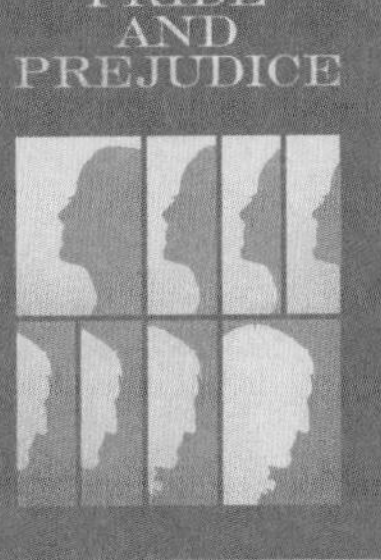

Jane Austen Cover to Cover

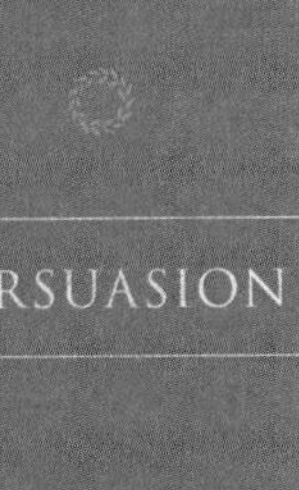

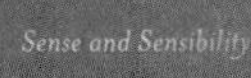

200 YEARS *of* CLASSIC COVERS

Margaret C. Sullivan

QUIRK BOOKS
PHILADELPHIA

All the images are courtesy the individual owners and the author except the following: Manuscript, Archives, and Rare Book Library, Emory University (pages 24–25); the Henry and Alberta Hirshheimer Burke Collection and the Winn Family Collection, Goucher College Special Collections (pages 12, 13, 14, 15, 16–17, 22, 23, 26, 28, 29, 36–37, 38, 40, 42, 48, 49, 51, 53, 54–55, 56–57, 60, 87, 146, 188, 189, 190, 191, 192, 194, 195, 196, 198, 199, 201).

The summaries are adapted from *The Jane Austen Handbook* by Margaret C. Sullivan (Quirk Books, 2007).

Library of Congress Cataloging in Publication Number: 2013957089
ISBN: 978-1-59474-725-0

Printed in China

Typeset in Caslon and Verlag
Editorial assistance by Blair Thornburgh
Designed by Andie Reid
Cover illustration (background) by Heads of State; cover design by Andie Reid
Production management by John J. McGurk

Quirk Books
215 Church Street
Philadelphia, PA 19106
quirkbooks.com

10 9 8 7 6 5 4 3 2 1

For my brother Bill
Who took me to the library, and then to the playground

Contents

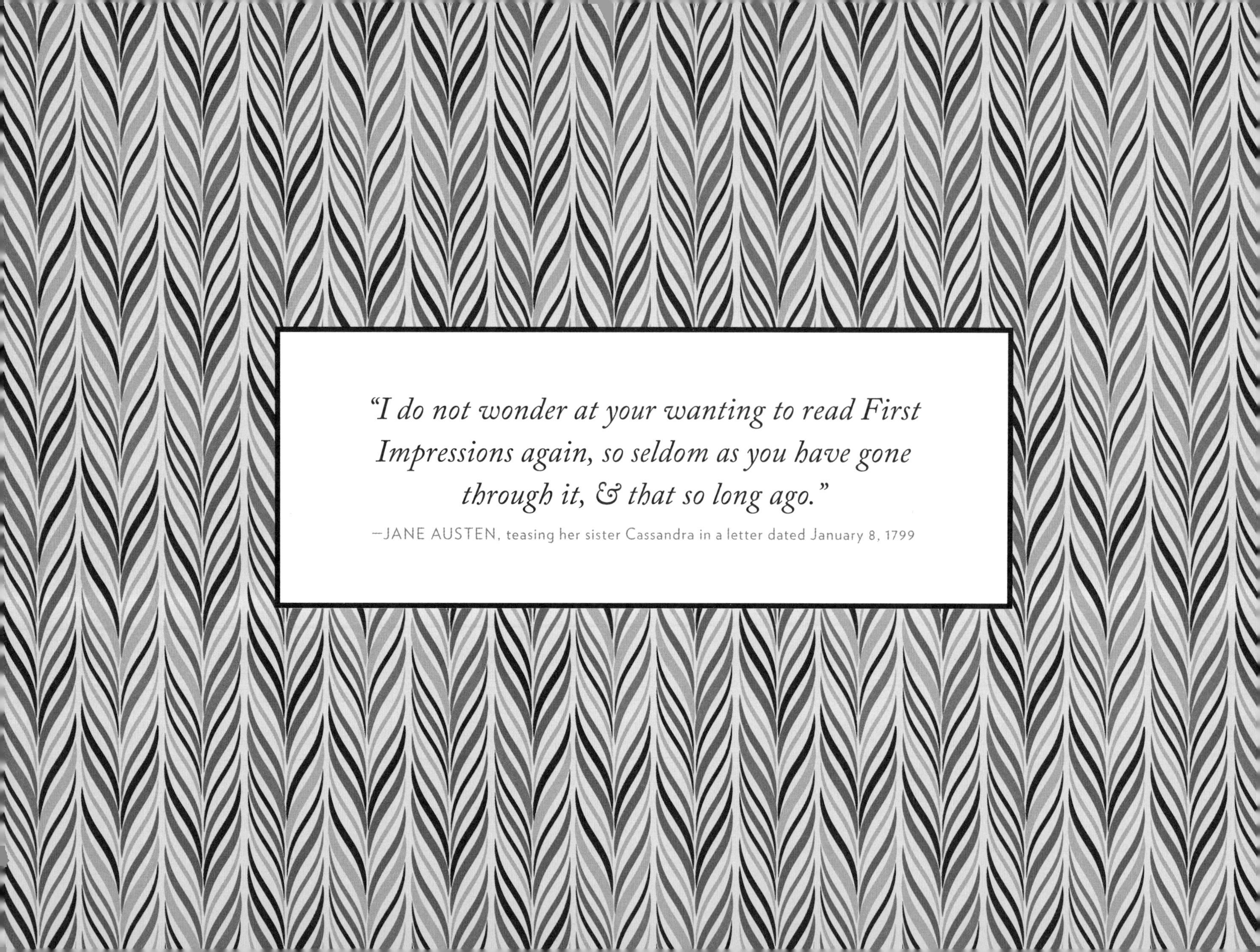

"I do not wonder at your wanting to read First Impressions again, so seldom as you have gone through it, & that so long ago."

—JANE AUSTEN, teasing her sister Cassandra in a letter dated January 8, 1799

INTRODUCTION

"First Impressions"

"Never judge a book by its cover." It's a saying so common that it has passed into cliché, and when it comes to Jane Austen, one endeavors to avoid cliché. Yet Austen initially referred to the book that would become her most famous—what we know today as *Pride and Prejudice*—by the title "First Impressions." Many an Austen heroine must learn to read other people better, beyond first impressions, and to know herself as well. Elizabeth Bennet, the writer's most beloved heroine, judged her relatives, her neighbors, and, certainly, Mr. Darcy, with his taciturn and unfriendly demeanor. So how can Janeites, trained in such a school, do any differently? If Austen teaches us anything, it is that first impressions are often false . . .

Perhaps you first encountered Jane Austen's work in a paperback edition, dog-eared from being jammed into a pocket or bag, striped with highlighting and crisscrossed with underlining and penciled marginalia. Or maybe you are a collector of fine editions, having invested in handsome matching hardbacks or weightier tomes bursting with scholarly commentary about the writer and the mores of Regency England. But it could be that you're still using those old paperbacks for your yearly reread, and there's not a thing wrong with that. No one shall judge your treasures.

The covers gathered in this volume represent two hundred years of publication, interpretation, marketing, and misapprehensions of Jane Austen's works, but underneath the variety of images one thing remains the same: the text that left the pen of a woman in Hampshire, England, two centuries ago. Austen's imagination and intellect transcended the fiction of her own time and created the cherished characters and timeless stories for which she is still celebrated today. No matter how beautiful, tacky, infuriating, beguiling, silly, or strange the packaging may be, the story inside never changes. And that, after all, is the most important thing.

But that doesn't mean that we, like Elizabeth Bennet, cannot be diverted by "follies and nonsense, whims and inconsistencies"; or fail to appreciate, like Marianne Dashwood, the natural beauty of a precious object; or, like Catherine Morland, simply enjoy a ripping good tale. For readers aplenty, there are no stories better than these. Follow along on a journey across the years, from the early 1800s to today, and from handset typography to digital technology, as each generation of Jane Austen fans interprets and experiences her works anew.

Chronology

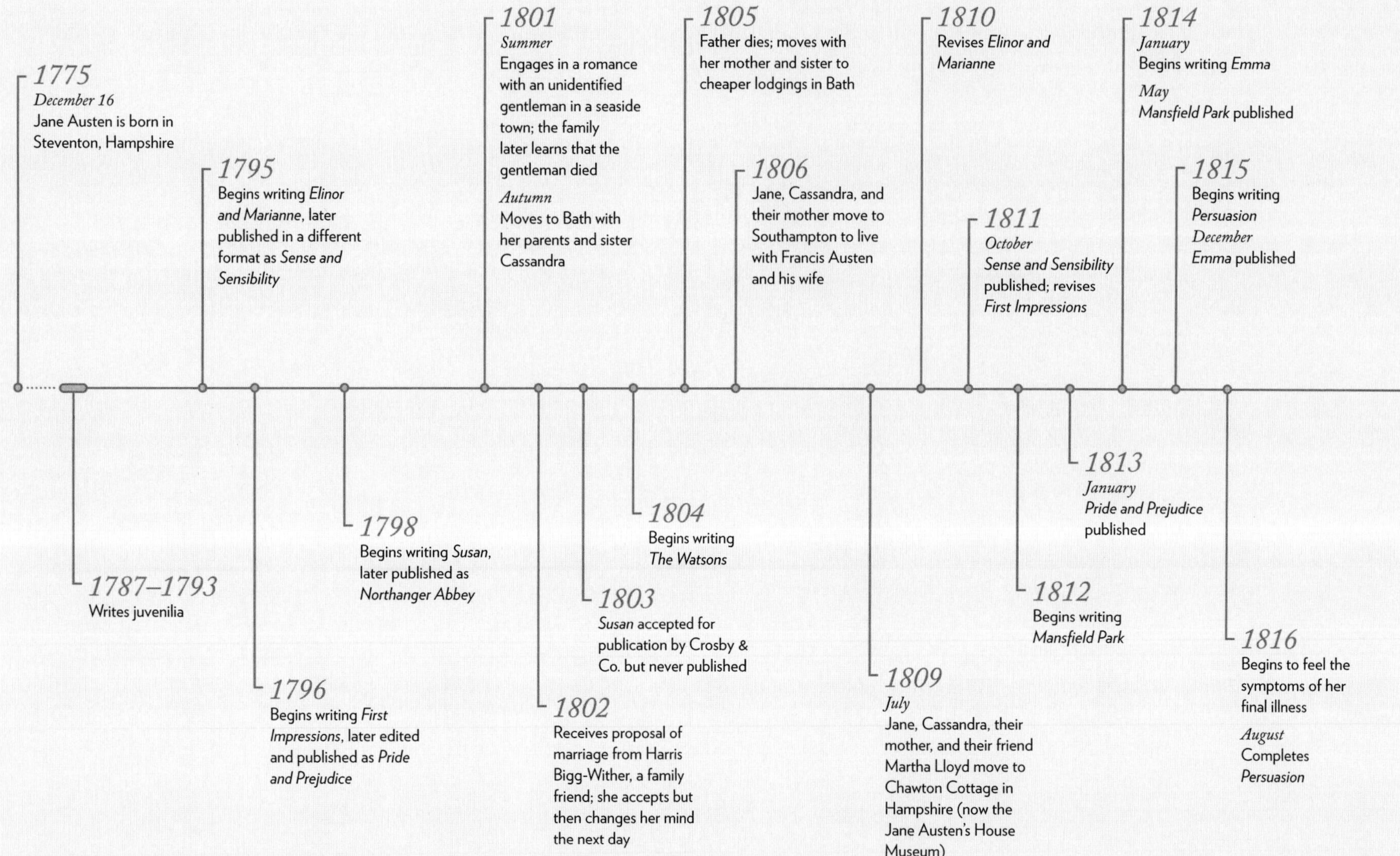

1775
December 16
Jane Austen is born in Steventon, Hampshire
1787–1793
Writes juvenilia
1795
Begins writing *Elinor and Marianne*, later published in a different format as *Sense and Sensibility*
1796
Begins writing *First Impressions*, later edited and published as *Pride and Prejudice*
1798
Begins writing *Susan*, later published as *Northanger Abbey*
1801
Summer
Engages in a romance with an unidentified gentleman in a seaside town; the family later learns that the gentleman died
Autumn
Moves to Bath with her parents and sister Cassandra
1802
Receives proposal of marriage from Harris Bigg-Wither, a family friend; she accepts but then changes her mind the next day
1803
Susan accepted for publication by Crosby & Co. but never published
1804
Begins writing *The Watsons*
1805
Father dies; moves with her mother and sister to cheaper lodgings in Bath
1806
Jane, Cassandra, and their mother move to Southampton to live with Francis Austen and his wife
1809
July
Jane, Cassandra, their mother, and their friend Martha Lloyd move to Chawton Cottage in Hampshire (now the Jane Austen's House Museum)
1810
Revises *Elinor and Marianne*
1811
October
Sense and Sensibility published; revises *First Impressions*
1812
Begins writing *Mansfield Park*
1813
January
Pride and Prejudice published
1814
January
Begins writing *Emma*
May
Mansfield Park published
1815
Begins writing *Persuasion*
December
Emma published
1816
Begins to feel the symptoms of her final illness
August
Completes *Persuasion*

1817

January
Begins writing *Sanditon*; last works on it in March

May
Goes with Cassandra to Winchester to seek medical care

July 18
Jane Austen dies

1818

December
Northanger Abbey and *Persuasion* published

1832

All six novels reblished as part of Bentley's Standard Editions

1869

J. E. Austen-Leigh's *Memoir of Jane Austen* published, renewing public interest in her novels

1923

R. W. Chapman publishes the *Oxford Illustrated Jane Austen*, the first scholarly treatment of Austen's novels, collated from early editions

1935

Helen Jerome's stage adaptation of *Pride and Prejudice* produced on Broadway

1938

Penguin publishes *Pride and Prejudice* as part of its Illustrated Classics series

BBC broadcasts a television play of *Pride and Prejudice*

1940

MGM releases a big-screen film adaptation of *Pride and Prejudice*

1980

BBC broadcasts a five-episode series of *Pride and Prejudice*

1995

Columbia Pictures releases a big-screen film adaptation of *Sense and Sensibility* starring Emma Thompson and Kate Winslet

Sony Pictures Classics releases a film adaptation of *Persuasion* starring Amanda Root and Ciaran Hinds

BBC broadcasts a new, enormously popular five-episode series of *Pride and Prejudice* starring Jennifer Ehle and Colin Firth

1996

A&E broadcasts the hugely popular new series of *Pride and Prejudice* in the US

Miramax releases *Emma* starring Gwyneth Paltrow

BBC broadcasts a new adaptation of *Emma* starring Kate Beckinsale

1997

A&E broadcasts the Kate Beckinsale adaptation of *Emma* in the US

1999

Miramax releases *Mansfield Park*

2005

Focus Features releases a big-screen adaptation of *Pride and Prejudice* starring Keira Knightley and Matthew Macfadyen

Cambridge University Press begins to publish its new, definitive editions of Austen's novels and other works

2007

ITV broadcasts three new television films of *Mansfield Park*, *Northanger Abbey*, and *Persuasion* in the UK

Amazon releases the Kindle, creating a new market for digital editions of Austen's work

2008

BBC broadcasts a new three-part series of *Sense and Sensibility*

PBS broadcasts a "Jane Austen Season" consisting of the new adaptations of *Mansfield Park*, *Northanger Abbey*, *Persuasion*, and *Sense and Sensibility*, as well as the 1995 adaptation of *Pride and Prejudice* and the 1997 adaptation of *Emma*

2009

BBC broadcasts a new series of *Emma* starring Romola Garai

2010

PBS broadcasts the new series of *Emma* in the US

2012

April
First episode of "The Lizzie Bennet Diaries" Web series, a contemporary adaptation of *Pride and Prejudice*, premieres on YouTube

"I want to tell you I have got my own darling child from London."

—JANE AUSTEN, speaking of *Pride and Prejudice*, to Cassandra Austen in a letter dated January 29, 1813

CHAPTER ONE
Her Own Darling Children

• 1811–1818 •

In November 1797 Jane Austen's father, the Reverend George Austen, wrote a letter to the London publisher Thomas Cadell offering him "a manuscript novel, comprising 3 vols." and inquiring about the cost of publishing the book at the author's risk. That manuscript was a novel by his younger daughter Jane that she called *First Impressions*. Despite Mr. Austen's hint that he would be willing to cover all related expenses, Cadell rejected the manuscript. Readers today know that passed-over best-selling novel as *Pride and Prejudice*, and we are grateful for its existence.

In Austen's time, several publishing models were available to authors. The one that she used most often was publishing on commission, which meant the publisher made all arrangements, paying production and advertising costs and taking a 10 percent commission on profits. This method could be lucrative but was more likely to be risky, for if the books did not sell, the author ended up owing money to the publisher.

The more prestigious (and common) publishing model was the outright sale of a book's copyright to the publisher. Copyright in the early nineteenth century was granted for fourteen years, renewable for a total of twenty-eight years. Authors preferred this method because payment was guaranteed, and the publisher assumed all risk; if the book was popular, however, the author received nothing more than the initial payment. The only book for which Austen sold the copyright was *Pride and Prejudice*.

In Austen's time the audience for novels was small, primarily the gentry and upper classes, most of whom borrowed novels rather than purchased them. The biggest customers were circulating libraries and book societies. Members of a circulating library paid a yearly fee (perhaps a guinea, or 21 shillings) for borrowing privileges; they generally could take out only a single volume, necessitating a trio of visits to read a novel, which usually appeared in three volumes. Some libraries—usually those in large cities—offered more expensive membership levels that allowed subscribers to borrow multiple volumes at a time. In the countryside, book societies took up the call. Members pooled their money to purchase books and then read them in turn. Jane and Cassandra Austen belonged to a book society in their village of Chawton, in Hampshire.

Despite the rejection by Cadell, Austen continued to write. In 1803 she sold the copyright of an epistolary novel she called *Susan* (later published as *Northanger Abbey*) to the publisher Crosby & Co. for ten pounds. The transaction makes Crosby seem an incredible cheapskate, but for an unknown novelist, such meager payment was typical. Crosby advertised the publication of *Susan* but then never followed through. When Austen attempted to force his hand by demanding he either publish the book or return the manuscript to her, Crosby replied that she could have her text for the ten pounds he had paid, a sum that was well beyond her means.

THOMAS EGERTON FIRST EDITION

SENSE AND SENSIBILITY

Jane Austen's father died in 1805, after which the Austen women—Jane, her mother, and her sister Cassandra—suffered a period of financial instability. Five of Jane's brothers contributed what they could (the sixth brother, George, had disabilities and was unable to help), and it was not until the summer of 1809 that the ladies had a permanent home. Jane's elder brother Edward had inherited three estates from a rich childless cousin, and he was able to give his mother and sisters a cottage in the village of Chawton, in Hampshire. Back in the peaceful country that she loved, and within the security of a new home, Austen dusted off the novels she had written years before. The first one, which she had originally called *Elinor and Marianne*, was retitled *Sense and Sensibility*. Austen had her brother Henry approach a publisher he knew in London, Thomas Egerton, who agreed to publish the novel on commission. Using Charles Roworth of London as printer, he ordered an initial print run of 750 copies. The novel appeared in 1811 as three volumes, as was typical for that time, and was sold for 15 shillings.

THOMAS EGERTON FIRST EDITION

PRIDE AND PREJUDICE

As *Sense and Sensibility* made its way into the world, Austen dusted off another novel to prepare it for publication: the book that her father had attempted to get published all those years before. She had called it *First Impressions*, but in the intervening years, another book by that title had come out. So Austen took a phrase from the final chapter of one of her favorite novels, *Cecilia* by Frances Burney, and called her work *Pride and Prejudice*. An alliterative pairing, as she'd done for her first novel, the title was possibly an early attempt at branding by an otherwise anonymous author. Austen's sister Cassandra later left notes indicating that Jane had made "additions and contractions" to the manuscript; Jane lightheartedly wrote in a letter that she had "lop't and crop't" the original (the longer manuscript does not survive).

Egerton offered to purchase the copyright of *Pride and Prejudice* for 110 pounds. Austen wrote to her friend Martha Lloyd that she would have preferred 150 pounds, but she settled for the guaranteed sum. She never received another payment for what would become one of the most popular novels in history. Egerton published *Pride and Prejudice* in 1813, maximizing his earnings by printing the three-volume book on cheaper paper, using smaller type (and thus less paper), and charging more for it: 18 shillings. The first edition of 1,000 copies sold out quickly, prompting him to run a second edition of 750 copies, followed by a third in two volumes, with the chapters renumbered.

THOMAS EGERTON SECOND EDITION

SENSE AND SENSIBILITY

Sense and Sensibility received several good reviews, and the book sold well enough to prompt publisher Thomas Egerton to purchase *Pride and Prejudice*. After *Pride and Prejudice* became a hit, its popularity rebounded on *Sense and Sensibility*, whose first edition finally sold out. In 1813 Egerton recommended a second edition.

THOMAS EGERTON FIRST EDITION

MANSFIELD PARK

Meanwhile, Austen was already working on her next novel, a completely new work. Having learned a hard lesson from *Pride and Prejudice*, to which she had relinquished her rights as author, this time Austen refused to sell the copyright. Furthermore, she insisted that Egerton, the publisher, print on even thinner paper and charge the same 18 shillings as he had for *Pride and Prejudice*. Despite the success of Austen's previous two novels, Egerton chose to print the first edition of *Mansfield Park*, which appeared in May 1814, in only 1,250 copies. The run sold out in six months. Austen wished to publish a second edition, but Egerton did not think it would sell. Nevertheless, a second U.K. edition was published in 1816, and a U.S. edition appeared in 1832 (see page 23).

Typical of the era, the original book is here rebound as a three-quarter-calf binding with marbled boards.

FIRST EDITION AND "PHILADELPHIA" EDITION

EMMA

Undaunted by Thomas Egerton's refusal to publish a second edition of *Mansfield Park*, Austen took her next novel, *Emma*, to an even more prestigious and fashionable company: John Murray, the publisher of Lord Byron and Walter Scott, two of the era's best-selling authors. Murray offered 450 pounds for the copyrights to *Emma*, *Mansfield Park*, and *Sense and Sensibility*. Having earned nearly 300 pounds on the first edition of *Mansfield Park* alone, Austen decided to publish on commission the first edition of *Emma* and the second edition of *Mansfield Park*. This initial edition of *Emma* (*right*), published in late 1815, had a run of 2,000 copies, of which 500 were remaindered (unsold) four years later.

Some copies of Austen's novels were exported from the United Kingdom to the United States. Because no reciprocal copyright-protection arrangement then existed between the two countries, American companies often reproduced and sold popular novels without compensating the author. In 1816 the Philadelphia publisher Mathew Carey published the first U.S. edition of Austen's novels—*Emma* appeared in two volumes (*far right*) and sold for $2.50. Meanwhile, back on the Continent, foreign-language editions of Austen's works began to appear, also without author payments or royalties. The fast-and-loose translations often changed the story at the translator's whim (see Chapter Six).

Above: John Murray first edition; *right*: Carey & Lea first edition

EMMA
EMMA
EMMA
1
2
3

EMMA
EMMA

JOHN MURRAY FIRST EDITION

NORTHANGER ABBEY & PERSUASION

Austen completed the manuscript of what would eventually be known as *Persuasion* in 1816. In addition, she had finally bought back the manuscript of *Susan* from Crosby & Co. In a delightful bit of schadenfreude, her brother Henry retrieved the manuscript and informed the publisher that the novel he had so scorned was by the author of the immensely popular *Pride and Prejudice*.

Because a novel titled *Susan* had been published in the meantime, Austen renamed her heroine Catherine and wrote an "advertisement," which she placed at the beginning of the book, to explain changes in the geography and habits of Bath since the time the novel was written. Though she apparently meant to publish the book, she set it aside, along with *Persuasion*.

By this time, symptoms of the illness that would eventually claim her life had begun to appear. In January 1817 Austen started a new novel about a sensible young lady on a visit to the seaside town of Sanditon. She completed eleven chapters before poor health forced her to stop in March. In the early morning of July 18, 1817, Jane Austen died in her sister's arms. She left a short will naming Cassandra her executor and principal heir. Once the estate was settled, Cassandra arranged for the two completed manuscripts to be published together in 1818 as a four-volume set. She and Henry retitled the novels *Persuasion* and *Northanger Abbey*. The set was priced at one pound four shillings, and the print run was 1,750 copies.

ON THE MAKING OF BOOKS

No, indeed, I am never too busy to think of S. and S. . . . I have had two sheets to correct, but the last only brings us to Willoughby's first appearance.

—JANE AUSTEN to her sister Cassandra in a letter dated April 25, 1811

In Jane Austen's time, the entire bookmaking process was done by hand. Once a book was accepted for publication, the printing stage swung into action. Type was set manually from the author's handwritten manuscript, with the composer correcting spelling and punctuation errors while placing rows of metal letters into page-sized holders called galleys. Since printers rarely had enough type to set an entire book at once, the composition was done in batches. Multiple book pages were printed on a single sheet, called a signature, which was then folded and cut to form the leaves in the proper sequence.

Austen's novels were *duodecimo* size, meaning that each standard printer's sheet was folded to make twelve leaves, producing a book about the size of a modern paperback (roughly 5 by 7¾ inches). Only a few sheets would be printed at a time, to allow for proofreading. After the author approved the printed copies, the printer would produce enough sheets for the entire print run, reset the type for the next sheets, print, proofread, and repeat until all sheets were printed. Most books appeared in three volumes, including all of Austen's novels published during her lifetime. To speed up the process, in some cases three different printers might each print one volume of a multivolume book.

The folded sheets, or gatherings, were then assembled into the final book and bound in a plain cardboard binding called "boards" (see example on page 15); a paper label with the book's title was pasted onto the spine. This rather plain presentation was not meant to last. Wealthier purchasers (the likes of Mr. Darcy, for example) would have the books rebound for the family library, using their own distinctive style so that all the volumes matched.

Among bindings, the most luxurious and expensive was full leather, either calf or morocco (goatskin). To save money, some owners would have a book bound half-calf, in which the front and back covers were bound with paper but the spine and corners were leather, combining good looks and improved durability. For quarter-calf binding, only the spine was covered in leather; in three-quarter-calf binding, the spine, corners, and a little of the front and back covers were leather bound.

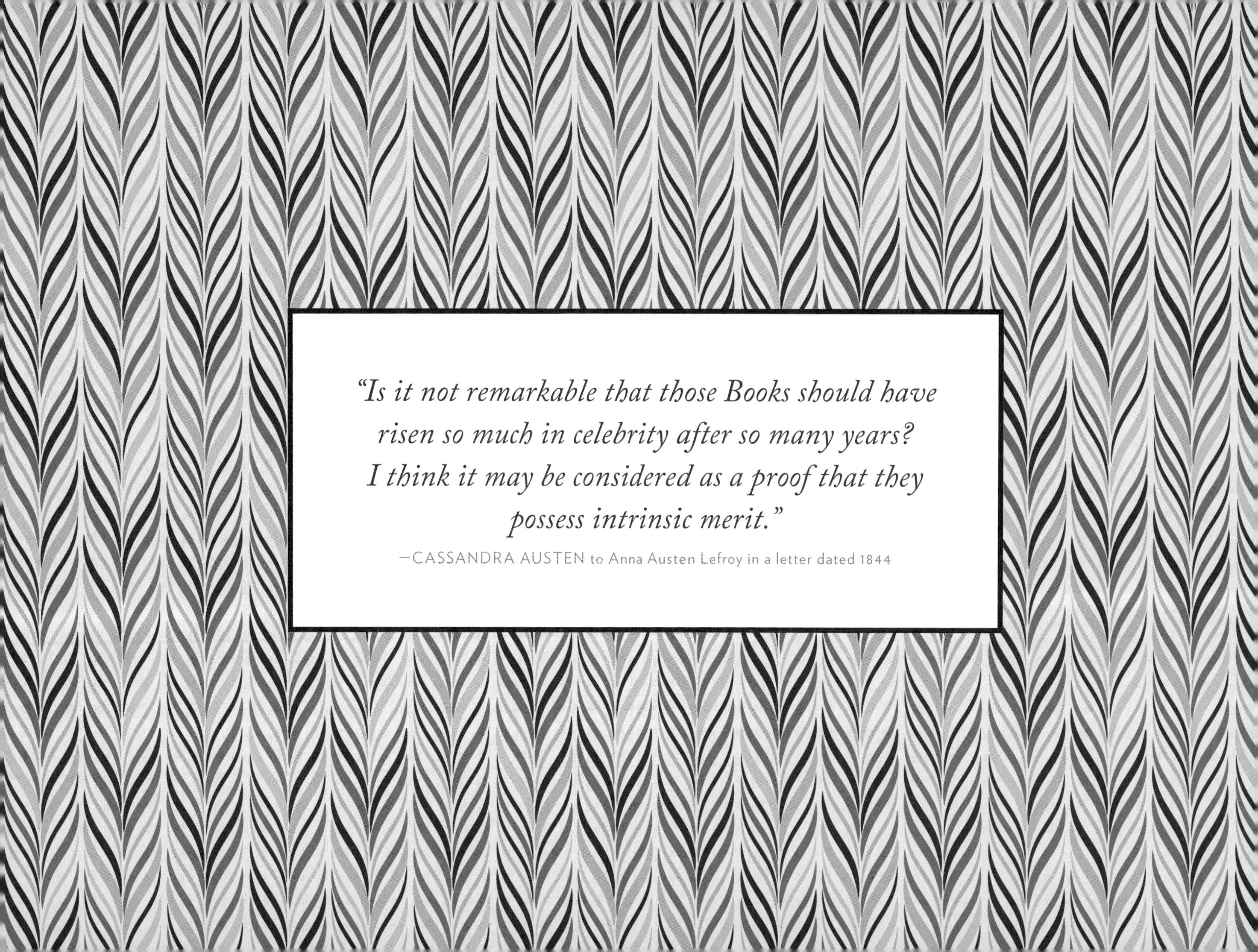

"Is it not remarkable that those Books should have risen so much in celebrity after so many years? I think it may be considered as a proof that they possess intrinsic merit."

—CASSANDRA AUSTEN to Anna Austen Lefroy in a letter dated 1844

CHAPTER TWO

Books of Intrinsic Merit

• 1832–1920 •

In 1817 Thomas Egerton remaindered *Sense and Sensibility* and the third edition of *Pride and Prejudice*. John Murray remaindered his unsold stock of *Emma* in 1820, and a year later he did the same for the second edition of *Mansfield Park* as well as the only editions of *Persuasion* and *Northanger Abbey*. And with that, only four years after her death, Jane Austen's books were out of print. But her work was not meant to slip into obscurity—other publishers would soon step up to supply the renascent demand.

Austen still had fans, both ordinary and famous and on both sides of the Atlantic. One admirer was Sir Walter Scott, who in 1826 confessed to his diary: "Read again, for the third time at least, Miss Austen's finely written novel of 'Pride And Prejudice.' That young Lady had a talent for describing the involvements and feelings and characters of ordinary life, which is to me the most wonderful I ever met with. . . . What a pity such a gifted creature died so early!" This bit of private praise reappeared in a memoir of Scott published in 1837, and Cassandra Austen even copied it in her own hand to keep.

But Scott's admiration wasn't mere flattery. His novels were the most popular books of the early nineteenth century, and they drove up demand for fiction, including the stories written by Austen. As literate populations grew, they became more urban and mobile; publishers catered to this burgeoning audience by producing cheaper books that the middle class could easily afford. With the mechanization of the printing process, production costs dropped and prices followed suit. Books were soon available everywhere and for everyone.

Ten years after remaindering his editions of Austen's books, the publisher John Murray apparently thought an audience still existed for them, and in 1831 he approached Cassandra Austen with an offer to purchase the copyrights for all of her sister's novels. Cassandra seemed interested and inquired about republishing the novels on commission, but the deal fell through. A year later, another publisher, Richard Bentley, put forth his own offer of 250 pounds, and this time a deal was brokered. The sum of 40 pounds was deducted to purchase the copyright of *Pride and Prejudice* from the heirs of Thomas Egerton, and Bentley then published all six of Austen's novels in five volumes—with *Persuasion* and *Northanger Abbey* together once again—as part of his Standard Novels series of well-known British works.

BENTLEY'S STANDARD EDITIONS

These small cloth-bound books printed in tiny type sold for six shillings each when they appeared in 1832. They brought Austen's romantic fiction to a wider audience among the emerging middle class and put her work on the same shelf as that of other prominent authors, including James Fenimore Cooper and, later, Charles Dickens. They were also the first editions to be illustrated: each volume contained two remarkably unattractive black-and-white depictions of the characters dressed in 1830s fashions.

The Bentley books were reprinted continually until 1869, with the price steadily decreasing and the bindings becoming increasingly attractive. For the period, this edition was the most popular of Austen's novels—but the books weren't without competition. Although a change in copyright law increased the protection period to forty-two years for *Emma*, *Northanger Abbey*, and *Persuasion*, copyrights for all of Austen's books had expired by 1860, and other publishers were free to join the fray—and soon did.

CAREY & LEA

On the other side of the Atlantic, the Philadelphia publisher Carey & Lea published all six of Jane Austen's novels in 1832 and 1833. Each was published in two volumes and sold for $2. The first to appear was *Pride and Prejudice*, which had a print run of 750 copies and did not name Austen as author; the others had print runs of 1,250 copies, and their title pages attributed the stories to one "Miss Austen." Because no reciprocal copyright law bound the United States and the United Kingdom, copyright was not violated with these publications.

Perhaps in anticipation of more Puritan tastes associated with American society, the Carey & Lea editions were gently bowdlerized. Characters who casually took the Lord's name in vain, proclaming "Good God!" or similar oaths, had their dialogue edited to exclamations of only the nonblasphemous kind.

CHAPMAN AND HALL SELECT LIBRARY OF FICTION

Train travel revolutionized life in England in the 1840s and 1850s and helped transform reading habits as well. A smooth ride in a well-lit compartment was a much more pleasant reading experience than could be had in a lurching horse-drawn carriage. Seeing an opportunity to fill a need in the market, around this time the bookseller W. H. Smith began placing bookstalls in railway stations. The books were sold cheap and frequently featured sensationalistic stories meant to appeal to low-brow tastes, although older titles were also available—their expired copyrights made them a bargain to publish.

Numbers from the Select Library of Fiction, published by Chapman and Hall, were bound in plain boards with a yellow-glazed paper cover that displayed colorful and lurid illustrations, with the characters dressed in contemporary clothing. These so-called yellowbacks were small (about 7 by 5 inches), easy to carry, and priced to sell at no more than two shillings sixpence each. They were the least expensive editions of Austen's novels to date, and their low cost and convenient positioning spread her work to a still wider audience: the railroad commuter. The 1872 cover of *Pride and Prejudice* here, showing a demure Lydia Bennet flirting with the militia officers in Brighton, is typical of the yellowback illustration style, as are the 1872 *Mansfield Park* and the 1870 *Sense and Sensibility.*

SELECT LIBRARY OF FICTION.

JANE AUSTEN'S NOVELS.

AUTHOR'S EDITION.

Price 2s. Picture Boards, or 2s. 6d. in Roxburghe.

SENSE AND SENSIBILITY.

PERSUASION, & NORTHANGER ABBEY.

MANSFIELD PARK.

PRIDE AND PREJUDICE.

EMMA.

"'Miss Austen's novels,' says Southey, 'are more true to nature, and have for my sympathies passages of finer feeling than any others of this age.' Sir Walter Scott and Archbishop Whately, in the earlier numbers of the *Quarterly Review*, called the attention of the public to their surpassing excellence."—*Quarterly Review*, [illegible], 1870.

"Shakespeare has neither equal nor second. But among the writers who have approached nearest to the manner of the great master, we have no hesitation in placing Jane Austen, a woman of whom England is justly proud."—*Lord Macaulay.*

[23] *SOLD BY ALL BOOKSELLERS.*

THE PEACOCK EDITION

In 1894 George Allen produced one of the first truly iconic editions of Austen's work. Now known as the Peacock Edition, the book's cover featured a stunning line drawing by Hugh Thomson, one of the most popular illustrators of his time. According to David Gilson's *Bibliography of Jane Austen*, the elaborate illustration was inspired by Macmillan's similarly decked-out New Cranford series of well-known British novels, but it's possible the designer may have taken inspiration from the book's hero, Mr. Darcy. (Though Austen mentions no peafowl at Darcy's estate, Pemberley, readers have imagined them there for years. Or perhaps a cheeky employee at George Allen was comparing the proud Darcy to the strutting bird.)

Thomson's 160 black-and-white illustrations for the Peacock Edition include scenes from the novel as well as decorative chapter titles and initials. Unlike the artists who designed the anachronistic yellowback editions, Thomson drew his settings and characters in styles appropriate to the Regency period in which the story was set. The book also contains an introduction by the critic George Saintsbury in which he coins the word "Janeites" (spelled "Janites" in his text). This beautifully rendered edition sold 25,000 copies over ten years, and it is prized by collectors even today, with copies selling for as much as $500.

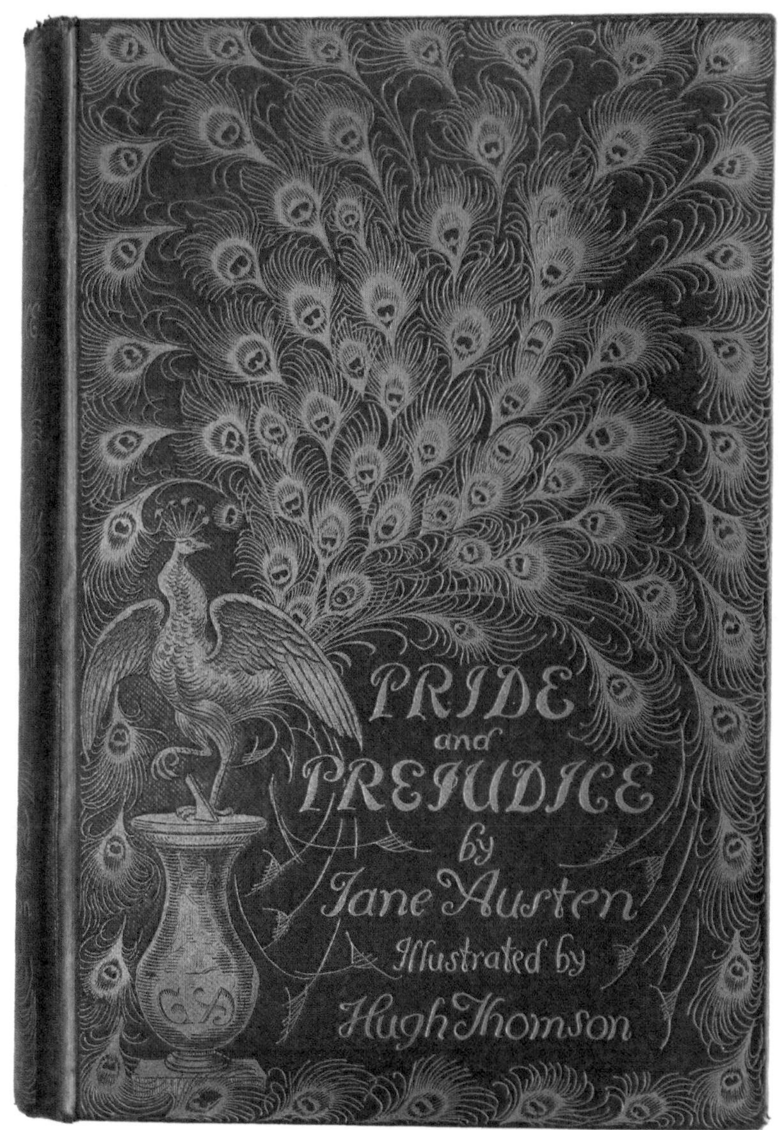

"You must allow me to tell you how ardently I admire and love you."

—Pride and Prejudice

HAMMOND ILLUSTRATED EDITIONS

When Hugh Thomson, illustrator of the Peacock Edition, turned his talents to drawing for the rest of the novels in Macmillan's Illustrated Editions of Jane Austen series, George Allen recruited Chris Hammond, one of the few female illustrators of the late nineteenth century, to take on Austen's remaining novels. This volume of *Sense and Sensibility* appeared in 1899. The Hammond Illustrated Editions share the beauty of the Peacock Edition, with their gold-tooled decorative covers in the Art Nouveau style. The artist's pen-and-ink drawings are similar to those of other late-nineteenth-century illustrated editions of Austen's works, though Hammond's are somewhat more detailed and perhaps may be described as showing a bit of a feminine touch. These volumes are relatively rare, and Hammond is not as celebrated among Janeites as Thomson is. Nevertheless, they are treasured and can fetch as much as $300 today.

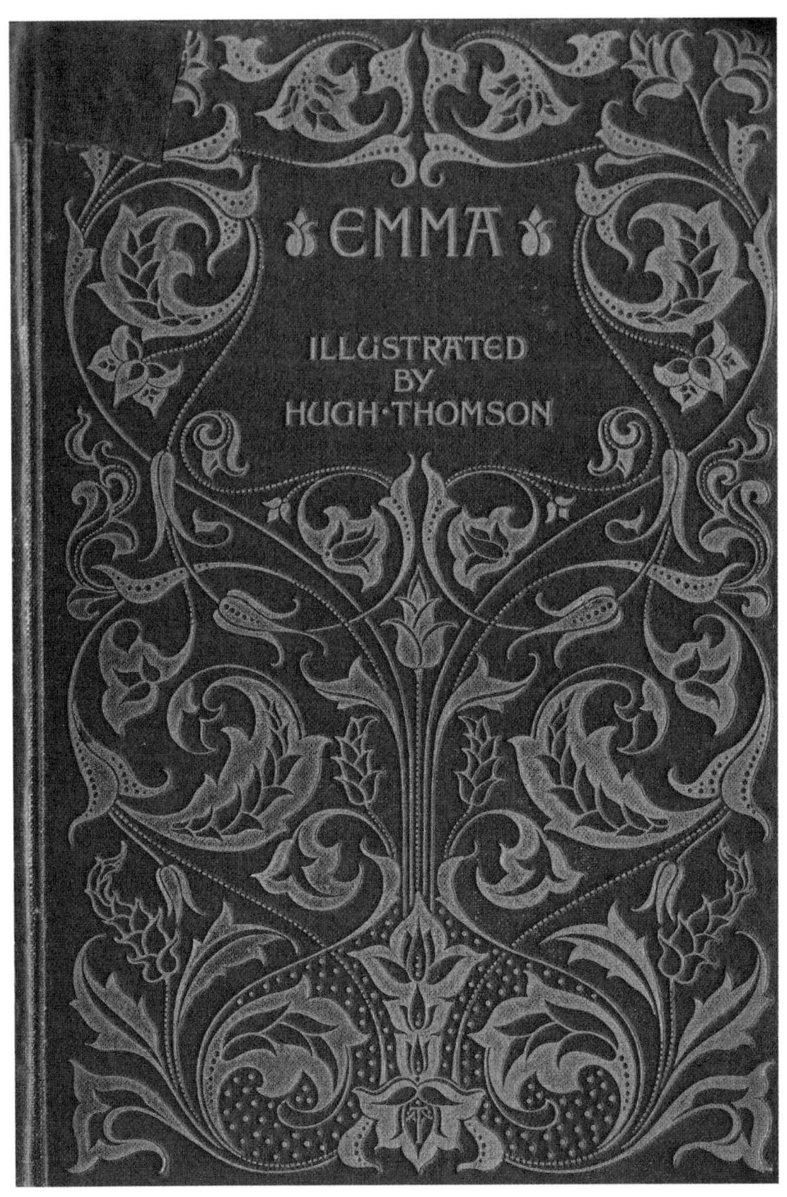

HUGH THOMSON ILLUSTRATED EDITION

Across the Atlantic, in 1896 the U.S. publisher Macmillan and Co. produced its own edition of *Pride and Prejudice*, featuring black-and-white line illustrations by Charles Brock. The book would go through six printings between 1895 and 1903. Like Thomson, Brock worked in fine pen-and-ink drawings that showed scrupulous attention to detail and correct period costumes, and the two illustrators are easily (and often) confused. Further complicating matters is the fact that Macmillan also published editions of Austen's other novels that featured illustrations by Thomson, including the edition of *Emma* at left. These were bound in red leather and included marbled endpapers.

"The person, be it gentleman or lady, who has not the pleasure in a good novel, must be intolerably stupid."

—Northanger Abbey

BROCK LITHOGRAPH EDITIONS

In 1892 the publisher J. M. Dent made an attempt at something of a scholarly edition of Austen's oeuvre: a ten-volume matched set that included introductions by the noted critic R. Brimley Johnson and featured illustrations by William C. Cooke. The set proved popular with audiences and was reprinted several times.

In 1898 Dent redesigned his editions, as shown at left. He took advantage of the new, cheaper printing technology called lithography, which used etched stones or metal plates to reproduce text and images. Cooke's drawings were replaced with new color illustrations by Charles Brock and his brother Henry: Henry ("H. M.") took on *Pride and Prejudice*, *Mansfield Park*, and *Northanger Abbey*, while Charles ("C. E.") drew for *Sense and Sensibility*, *Emma*, and *Persuasion*. Each of the four longer books published during Austen's lifetime was presented in two volumes, and the two posthumous books appeared as one volume each. Because color illustrations cost considerably more than black and white, the books contained only six apiece. Fortunately, the Brocks took their task seriously: they purchased eighteenth-century furniture and clothing for their models to pose with, which lends the images a perfect air of verisimilitude, not to mention longevity. The books have become collector's editions and can command prices of up to $200.

BROCK WATERCOLOR EDITIONS

Between 1907 and 1909 J. M. Dent published yet another set of all six Austen novels as part of its Series of English Idylls, which included well-known novels by such British authors as Elizabeth Gaskell, Oliver Goldsmith, and George Eliot. For this series Dent chose books for their ability to evoke a simpler time and the old-fashioned country life of England.

Each of Austen's novels was published as a single volume, complete with an elaborate gilt-embossed cover, beautiful "Wedgwood-style" title pages, illuminated endpapers, and pictures; these were supplied by Charles Brock (also of Dent's lithographic editions, page 31), who produced 24 watercolor paintings per title. Though these editions were reprinted several times throughout the early twentieth century, not all were bound in elaborate covers and endpapers, and they often omitted a few illustrations as well. Still, the books are truly heirloom quality, and collectors today continue to seek them out.

Until the appearance of these late-Victorian versions, all the editions of Austen's novels were intended for the general reader. Now, however, her books were being reimagined, redesigned, and purposely crafted into beautiful, collectible objects. But nothing gold can stay. As we shall see in the next chapter, with the end of the First World War, a new generation of readers was about to arrive on the scene, prompting publishers and editors to pursue a different direction to keep the books fresh.

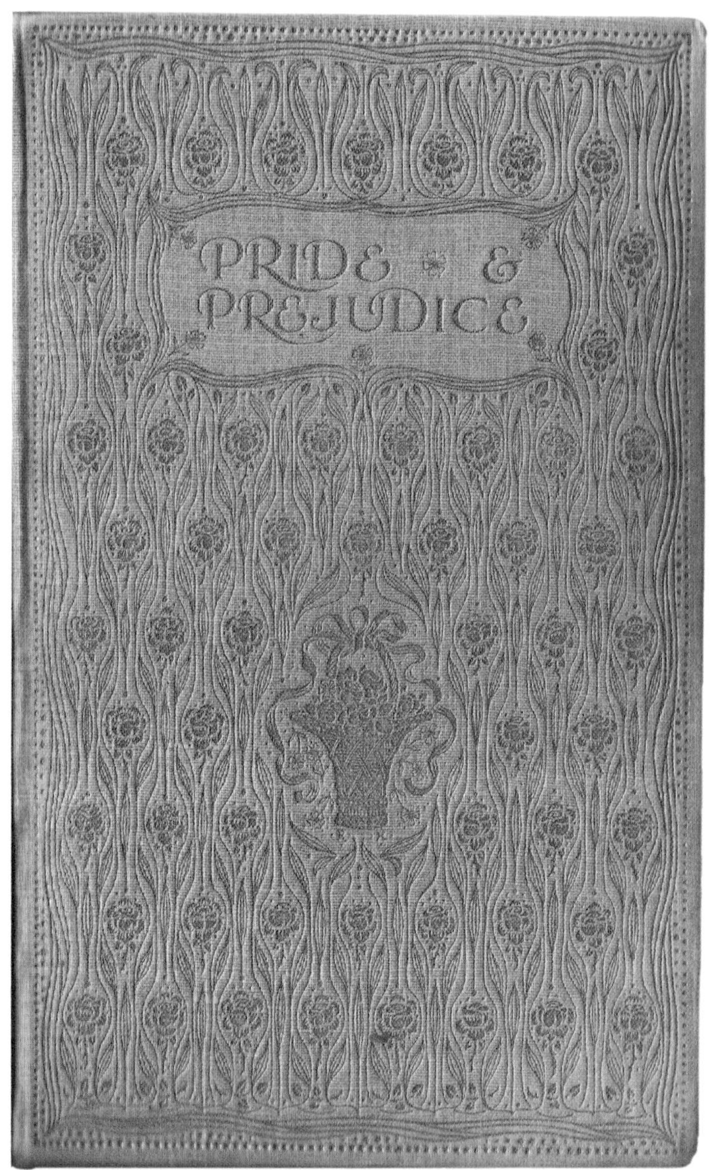

AUSTEN'S AMERICAN FANS

It was most gratifying also to receive a further proof of the high estimation in which my late sister's works are held by yourself and near connections, and to be further assured that her talent as an authoress was duely appreciated on the other side of the Great Atlantic; such testimony affords reasonable expectation that her name will be well known long after the present generation has passed away, wherever the English language is spoken or understood.

—SIR FRANCIS AUSTEN to Eliza Quincy in a letter dated May 19, 1863

In 1852 Eliza Susan Quincy, daughter of Josiah Quincy III, the president of Harvard University and a member of the prominent Boston family, wrote to Admiral Sir Francis Austen, Jane Austen's only surviving sibling. Ever one to curate an impressive social circle, Miss Quincy explained that John Marshall, chief justice of the Supreme Court, had introduced her to Austen's work, and that the rear admiral Ralph Randolph Wormeley of the Royal Navy had given her Sir Francis's address. Shameless name-dropping dispatched with, she went on to inform Austen's relatives that the author did have fans in the United States, and she primly requested "more information relative to her life than is given in the brief memoir prefixed to her works," assuring Sir Francis that "the autograph of his sister, or a few lines in her handwriting, would be placed among our chief treasures."

Sir Francis returned a gracious letter stating his pleasure that his sister's work was enjoyed in America. He shared not only some reminiscences of Jane but also a letter in her hand—written to her close friend Martha Lloyd, who had become Sir Francis's second wife some years after Jane's death.

Miss Quincy, to her credit, kept her end of the bargain and treasured the letter, as did the rest of her family. Upon hearing about it, her sister Anna Waterston wrote excitedly, "If the house catches fire to night,—please save the letter." In 1856 Anna and her family traveled to England to visit Sir Francis and enjoyed an afternoon in the company of his family at their home in Portsmouth. Sir Francis continued his correspondence with Miss Quincy until his death in 1865. The breathlessly enthusiastic correspondence, now held by the Massachusetts Historical Society, reveals a definite stateside cult of Jane Austen even before the British publication of Austen's nephew's *Memoir* in 1869. At the time, Jane's U.S. fan base was a who's who of elites, from socialites to the intelligentsia, but they were far from stiff and reserved in their admiration. When it came to their favorite novelist, Victorian Janeites were every bit as giddy as today's millennials.

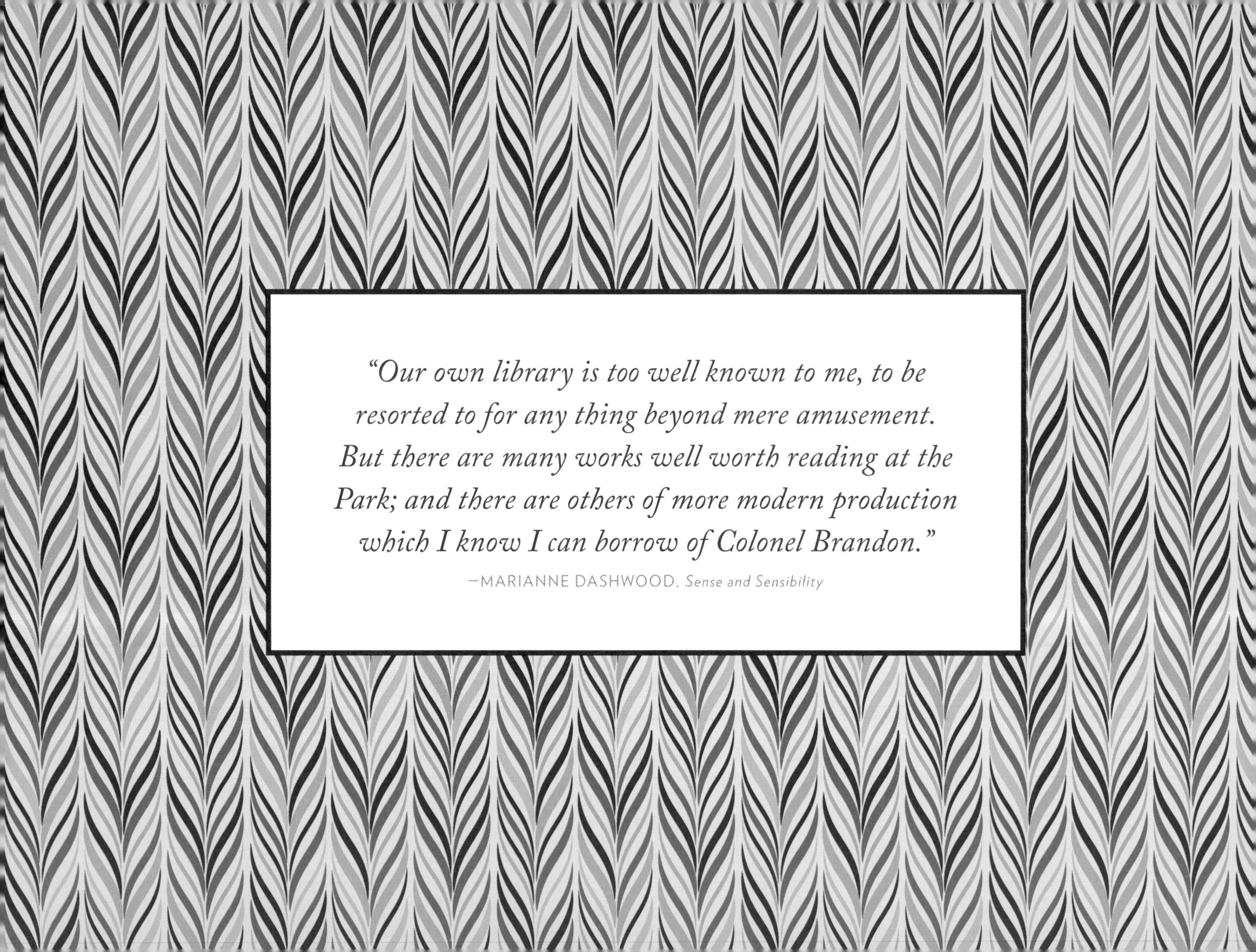

"Our own library is too well known to me, to be resorted to for any thing beyond mere amusement. But there are many works well worth reading at the Park; and there are others of more modern production which I know I can borrow of Colonel Brandon."

—MARIANNE DASHWOOD, *Sense and Sensibility*

CHAPTER THREE

Works of a More Modern Production

• 1920–1989 •

As the world heaved into the conflicts that would define the early twentieth century, Jane Austen—or her writing, at least—was drafted into service. During World War I, British soldiers took her books into the trenches and barracks, and those who later suffered from shell-shock were often advised to read her novels to calm their nerves. Her stories, full of humor and free from melodrama, represented aspects of British society that the war had ripped away. And for the first time, a true scholarship of her oeuvre began to emerge.

One of the returning soldiers was a former editor named R. W. (Robert) Chapman. As Austen's novels were published and republished, various editors had introduced errors, modernizations, and other noncanonical changes into the text. Chapman, an Oxford graduate and classical scholar, set out to edit the original texts with a scholar's eye. He assembled the editions printed during and just after the author's lifetime and collated them into the definitive edition of Austen's novels.

All great inventions arise from necessity, and such is true of the paperback. The idea was the brainchild of Allen Lane, an editor at the Bodley Head, who was having a hard time finding a cheap, decent read at his local railway station. Paperback books were not unknown at this time, but they had never gained popularity, being either too expensive or not of high literary quality. Lane created a simple design and reprinted good fiction by such popular authors as Agatha Christie and Ernest Hemingway, priced at six shillings. He was able to do so profitably because of the same technology that had advanced the printing process since Austen's day. Paper was now mass produced from pulped wood rather than cotton, and type was no longer set by hand but by machines. The invention of the rotary printing press in the mid-nineteenth century delivered printed material faster and in bulk. Lane's Penguin Books—sold in vending machines in nontraditional outlets like newsagents and train stations—were an immediate success and soon sparked a publishing revolution.

Not to be left behind in the book trade, the United States was gathering steam. In 1939 Pocket Books began to produce mass-market paperbacks. Its founder, Robert Fair DeGraff, had come to the conclusion that the threshold for turning a profit was 25 cents—an impossible price for a hardback. DeGraff was able to cut production costs by running his press overtime, gluing (rather than stitching) book pages, and reducing the books' trim size to 6½ by 4¼ inches—perfect for a pocket. Wary of the stigma attached to cheap softcover novels, DeGraff hired the scholar Philip Van Doren Stern to curate his first collection of titles, and by year's end Pocket Books had sold 1.5 million copies. With the thriftiness of the Great Depression and the shortages necessitated by another world war, affordable luxuries (and distractions) were in high demand. Paperback fiction fit the bill.

R. W. CHAPMAN EDITIONS

Unlike the novels published earlier by Macmillan and J. M. Dent (pages 28–29), R. W. Chapman chose to accompany Austen's text with period illustrations, such as fashion plates, contemporary prints, and drawings of carriages. Recent scholars have criticized Chapman's editorial work for being too heavy-handed—and for his reuse of material from a 1912 edition of *Pride and Prejudice* edited by Katherine Metcalfe, who would later become Chapman's wife, without noting her contribution—but most agree that his work was a boon to later generations. Nearly all subsequent texts have owed a debt to this edition.

Chapman's editions were also reused by his own publisher, Oxford University Press. This sweet little 1929 copy of *Pride and Prejudice* (*right*), for instance, was just small enough to slip into a pocket and included an introduction by Chapman. This shocking red 1930 edition of *Persuasion* is part of the publisher's World's Classics line that is still published today. The back cover copy charmingly describes the series as "in constant progress" so that "the general reader can build up a library of those books which, having become a part of himself, he wishes now to make a part of his home."

Though Austen had been dead for more than a century by the time this series appeared, some of her remaining unpublished manuscripts had trickled out over the years. In 1954, R. W. Chapman collected Austen's juvenile productions, unfinished works, and other pieces in a volume titled *Minor Works*, included thereafter with the *Oxford Illustrated Jane Austen*.

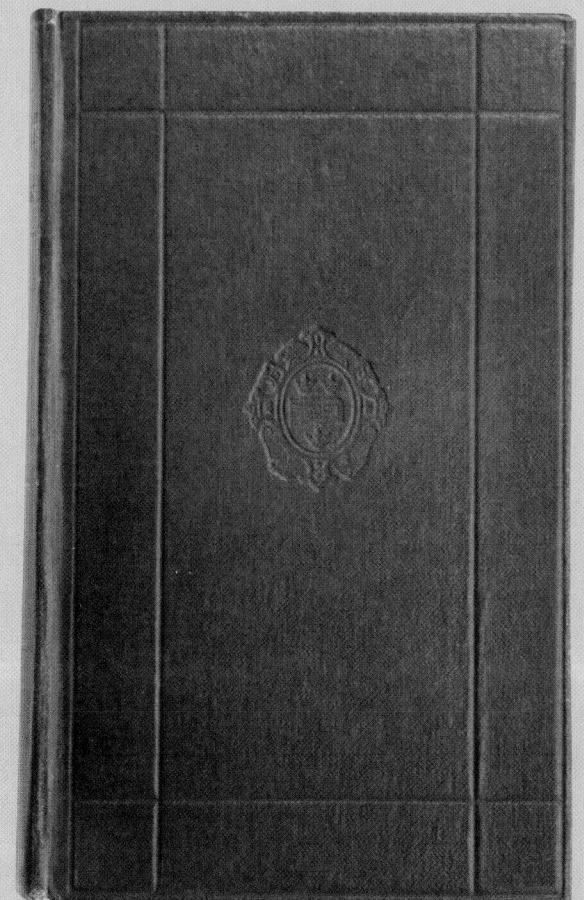

PERSUASION

JANE AUSTEN

THE WORLD'S CLASSICS

THE OXFORD ILLUSTRATED

JANE AUSTEN

EDITED BY

R·W·CHAPMAN

ELKIN MATHEWS & MARROT

This hint of a novel—only five chapters' worth—was left untitled and unfinished by Austen. She likely began writing it about 1803, while the family was living in Bath, and abandoned it after the death of her father, in 1805. Its title was supplied by her nephew James Edward Austen-Leigh when he published it as part of his 1871 biography *A Memoir of Jane Austen*. Over the years several writers have set about completing the novel, including this 1928 version written by Edith (great-granddaughter of Jane Austen's elder brother Sir Francis Austen) and Francis Brown. Far from being the first attempt, it is not even the first by one of Frank's descendants—his daughter Catherine Anne Hubback had published her completion of *The Watsons* back in 1850. This cover image displays a rather plain line drawing of a Regency-era lady and gentleman, surrounded by swoops and scrolls, and is accompanied by what appears to be a hand-lettered title. In addition to this work, Edith and her father, John Henry Hubback, wrote *Jane Austen's Sailor Brothers*, a biography of the novelist's brothers Sir Francis and Charles, both officers in the Napoleonic-era Royal Navy.

"He seems to have most engaging manners!" said Emma. "Well, we shall see how irresistible Mr. Tom Musgrave and I find each other."

MAXIMILIEN VOX ILLUSTRATED EDITIONS

Following in the tradition of its great Brock-illustrated editions of the late nineteenth and early twentieth centuries, in the 1930s J. M. Dent & Sons published a new set of Austen's novels that included seven or eight full-color plates by Maximilien Vox (1894–1974). Vox, a French cartoonist and historian of typography, had a spare style that emphasized a sketchy line from which the muted watercolor washes and sepia tone do not detract. Like many other illustrators, Vox took liberties with details of dress and appearance, few of which are specifically provided in the text. The volumes were assembled with as much care as the earlier editions, with endpapers decorated in superimposed J's and A's, an illustrated dust jacket, and an eye-catching harlequin-esque motif on the hardcover, shown here. This 1933 edition of *Pride and Prejudice* was republished in 1938.

PENGUIN ILLUSTRATED CLASSICS

Pride and Prejudice was the first Austen novel published by Penguin as part of its Penguin Illustrated Classics line, in 1938. All the books in this series were no longer under copyright, and Penguin used the money saved on author royalties to add illustrations—in this case, woodblock engravings by Helen Binyon (1904–1979), who is credited on the cover. Binyon chose to depict a scene from the novel, showing not the usual romantic exchange between main characters but, rather, a moment of departure. Perhaps it is Jane Bennet setting off for her fateful ride to Netherfield. Set between horizontal blocks of type announcing title and author, and flanked by vertical red bands, the bold image creates a dramatic effect that hints at the story within.

Jane was therefore obliged to go on horseback, and her mother attended her to the door with many cheerful prognostics of a bad day.

—Pride and Prejudice

POCKET BOOKS

In 1940 the bargain publisher Pocket Books produced this amusing, simplistic cover of a man's hand placing a wedding ring on a woman's finger. It is an inexpensive edition, meant for a general audience, unlike R. W. Chapman's earlier scholarly collation, which appeared beginning in the 1920s (page 36). This distinction between popular commercial editions of Austen's novels and those meant for the educational market would become more pronounced in the years after World War II.

ELIZABETH BENNET: *"You could not have made the offer of your hand in any possible way that would have tempted me to accept it."*

Pride and Prejudice
JANE AUSTEN
"One of the few great novels of the world."
—WILLIAM LYON PHELPS
COMPLETE AND UNABRIDGED
Pocket BOOK EDITION

AVALON PRESS

This 1949 edition features illustrations by Blair Hughes-Stanton, including a dust jacket image of two young ladies wearing a mish-mash of eighteenth- and nineteenth-century fashions: dropped waists instead of the traditional empire style, and hairstyles that are more Victorian than Regency. Such anachronisms were once a matter of course. In fact, publishers at this time felt no need to reflect details accurate to the setting. Many were content with images that merely conveyed a flavor of "the past"—whatever past they imagined it to be.

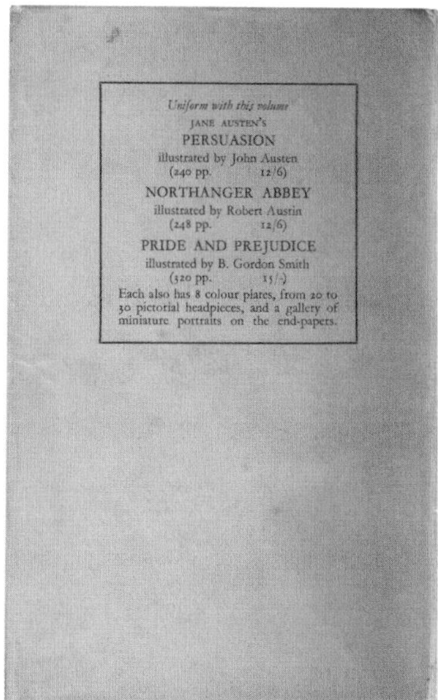

Each volume in this series is illustrated by a different artist.

ABBEY CLASSICS

Mr. Elton's tipsy Christmas Eve marriage proposal to Emma Woodhouse is perhaps an unusual choice for a cover illustration—one would suppose the hero might make an appearance in such a prominent image. But it does give the artist of this circa-1950 edition the scope to put the couple in a romantic clinch that brings out all the stylistic clichés of midcentury romances. As with the art that graced the editions published by Avalon Press (page 43), this illustration for John Murray's Abbey Classics line is far from appropriate for the period. Despite a few neck ruffles in a nod to the past, Emma's neat coif, broad-shouldered blouse, and waspish waist have more in common with a plucky Girl Friday than a heroine of Austen's time. The village of Highbury, too, appears to have been relocated to the Swiss Alps, judging by the peek of snowy trees and rooftop chalets seen through the carriage window.

Jane Austen finds herself in good company, with the likes of *Moby-Dick* and *Little Women*.

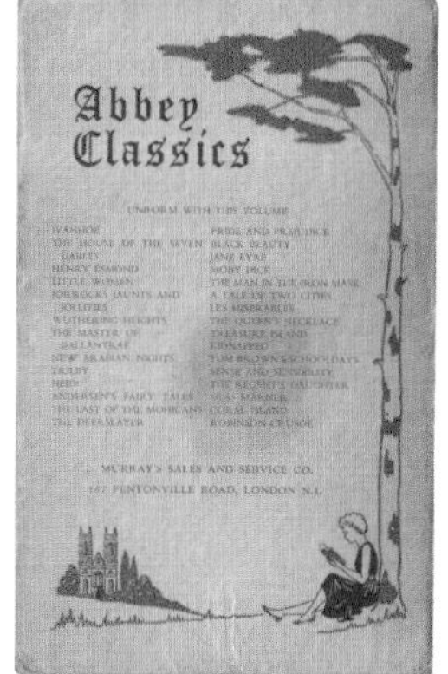

Abbey Classics

UNIFORM WITH THIS VOLUME

IVANHOE	PRIDE AND PREJUDICE
THE HOUSE OF THE SEVEN GABLES	BLACK BEAUTY
HENRY ESMOND	JANE EYRE
LITTLE WOMEN	MOBY DICK
JORROCKS' JAUNTS AND JOLLITIES	THE MAN IN THE IRON MASK
WUTHERING HEIGHTS	A TALE OF TWO CITIES
THE MASTER OF BALLANTRAE	LES MISERABLES
NEW ARABIAN NIGHTS	THE QUEEN'S NECKLACE
TRILBY	TREASURE ISLAND
HEIDI	KIDNAPPED
ANDERSEN'S FAIRY TALES	TOM BROWN'S SCHOOLDAYS
THE LAST OF THE MOHICANS	SENSE AND SENSIBILITY
THE DEERSLAYER	THE REGENT'S DAUGHTER
	SILAS MARNER
	CORAL ISLAND
	ROBINSON CRUSOE

MURRAY'S SALES AND SERVICE CO.
PENTONVILLE ROAD, LONDON N.1

RIVERSIDE EDITIONS

The fine folks at Houghton Mifflin in charge of the Riverside Editions in 1957 managed to make this student edition attractive through a dynamic cover image. Wedged between maroon trapezoids, a simple yet effective line drawing shows two young ladies, perhaps Emma Woodhouse and Harriet Smith, standing outside a Tudor-style dwelling. Like a peek into its pages, the black-and-white artwork seems to invite us into the book beyond. Yet the most valuable element of this edition is its introduction by the famed critic and professor Lionel Trilling, whose writings about Austen are held in great regard by many Janeites.

As a walking companion, Emma had very early foreseen how useful she might find her. . . . a Harriet Smith, therefore, one whom she could summon at any time to a walk, would be a valuable addition to her privileges.

NORTON LIBRARY

W. W. Norton & Co. created the Norton Library series for student editions, which meant that a scholarly look was preferred over prettiness. This drawing—a sketch, really—for a 1958 edition of *Persuasion* shows the Circus in Bath, the city where part of the novel is set, and nothing more. The text and some of the supplemental material are taken from the *Oxford Illustrated Jane Austen* (as stated on the back cover, below).

The image on the back cover is the infamous "wedding ring portrait," a pastiche of Cassandra Austen's watercolor of her sister (see sidebar, page 71).

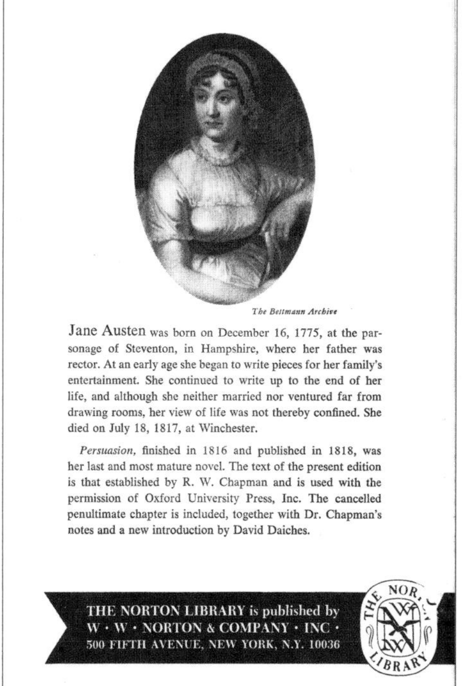

The Bettmann Archive

Jane Austen was born on December 16, 1775, at the parsonage of Steventon, in Hampshire, where her father was rector. At an early age she began to write pieces for her family's entertainment. She continued to write up to the end of her life, and although she neither married nor ventured far from drawing rooms, her view of life was not thereby confined. She died on July 18, 1817, at Winchester.

Persuasion, finished in 1816 and published in 1818, was her last and most mature novel. The text of the present edition is that established by R. W. Chapman and is used with the permission of Oxford University Press, Inc. The cancelled penultimate chapter is included, together with Dr. Chapman's notes and a new introduction by David Daiches.

THE NORTON LIBRARY is published by
W · W · NORTON & COMPANY · INC ·
500 FIFTH AVENUE, NEW YORK, N.Y. 10036

Midcentury Jane

In retrospect, the 1960s and 1970s seem almost too hip for Jane Austen. The postwar world brought an expansion of educational opportunities and new approaches to studying literature. The classical tradition was scorned in favor of the minimalist New Criticism, which concentrated solely on the text and excluded historical or biographical context. Meanwhile, paperback readership—especially among women—was skyrocketing, thanks to the advent of romance publishers such as Harlequin and Silhouette. Appearing monthly in groups of five or six "series," these short love stories bore similar cover designs and illustration styles (and, some would say, narrative content) so that readers could easily identify their favorite brand: contemporary stories of working girls falling for brooding bosses (nurses were especially popular) or so-called Gothic romances that intertwined mystery, danger, and Byronic heroes.

Austen's books were repackaged to suit the trend. Original cover illustrations featured scenes from the book in a literal and representational, albeit not historically accurate, way. Even books meant for the educational market needed to appeal to the modern (that is, teenage) student. Some editions presented the familiar staid and serious feel, whereas other designers borrowed the bright and bold visual vocabulary of the burgeoning school of Pop Art for a mod look. The covers on the following pages were doubtless once as hip and groovy as their readers but may appear quaint to us modern folks. Still, they provide an interesting chapter in the story of Austen's oeuvre.

SIGNET CLASSIC

This 1961 edition of *Pride and Prejudice* favors stylized fashion illustrations and a marvelously curled hairdo—Lydia would love it—to suggest a lively read. The accompanying drawings tease out details from the story (albeit symbolically—there's that peacock again!) and convey a classic story with a modern (well, modern at the *time*) twist. Contrast this look with the more serious Signet editions that would follow in the 1980s and 1990s (pages 64 and 88).

MR. BENNET: *"The officers will find women better worth their notice. Let us hope, therefore, that her being there may teach her her own insignificance. At any rate, she cannot grow many degrees worse without authorizing us to lock her up for the rest of her life."*

WASHINGTON SQUARE PRESS

Most Janeites consider *Mansfield Park* anything but a "frolicking comedy of manners," as the 1962 cover of this book declares. It is Austen's most serious novel, and not a favorite of some, though those who do love the story defend it fiercely. Even such determined partisans, however, must look askance at the description on the cover of this book. Likewise, the swooping text and zanily colorful impressionistic illustration seem a bit free-love for an Austen novel. And what, pray tell, is on Fanny Price's head?

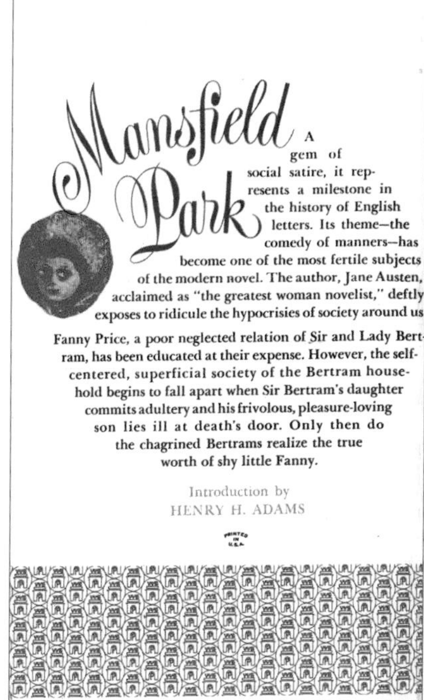

Mansfield Park

A gem of social satire, it represents a milestone in the history of English letters. Its theme—the comedy of manners—has become one of the most fertile subjects of the modern novel. The author, Jane Austen, acclaimed as "the greatest woman novelist," deftly exposes to ridicule the hypocrisies of society around us.

Fanny Price, a poor neglected relation of Sir and Lady Bertram, has been educated at their expense. However, the self-centered, superficial society of the Bertram household begins to fall apart when Sir Bertram's daughter commits adultery and his frivolous, pleasure-loving son lies ill at death's door. Only then do the chagrined Bertrams realize the true worth of shy little Fanny.

Introduction by
HENRY H. ADAMS

Set within a circular outline, the back cover text declares the book "a gem of social satire."

CAMPUS CLASSICS

It's *Psychedelic Pride and Prejudice*! With its heavy-lashed heroine and mop-topped hero, this Scholastic Books cover doesn't so much say seventies as scream it. The rainbow stripe and multiple-exposure sequence of profiles only add to the effect. Even the back cover copy evokes the decade's innocent yet racy subtext. A package that panders so obviously to teenagers may seem amusing in retrospect, but publishers haven't exactly stopped doing it (and probably never will).

The simplistic summary of the plot is offset by the serious quote from Somerset Maugham.

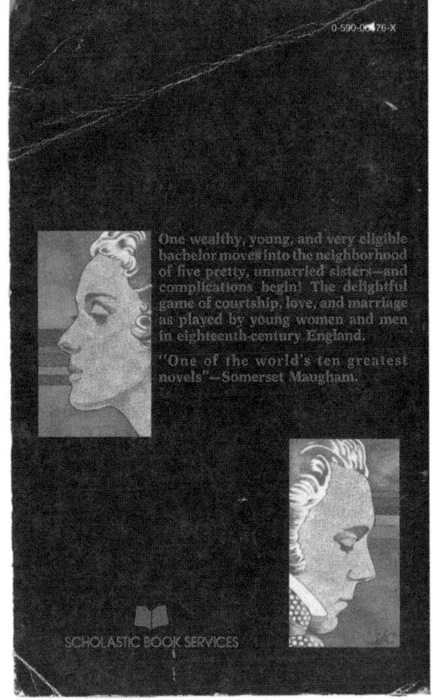

COLLIER BOOKS

This 1967 cover image manages the remarkable feat of existing simultaneously in both the nineteenth and the twentieth centuries. The silhouettes have a marvelous period-correct feel, but the contrasting colors are wholly modern in tone and emotional charge. That the introduction to the book was written by Elizabeth Stevenson is ironic in a geeky Janeite way. According to the (fictional) blurb from the Baronetage in the first chapter of *Persuasion*, Elizabeth Stevenson was the maiden name of Anne Elliot's mother.

ARROW CLASSICS

The adorable cover illustration for this 1967 Airmont Publishing Company edition of *Mansfield Park* perfectly describes the scene in which Fanny Price rests outside while visiting Mr. Rushworth's estate at Sotherton. "I shall soon be rested," said Fanny, "to sit in the shade on a fine day, and look upon verdure, is the most perfect refreshment." The illustrator has eliminated Mary Crawford from the equation, while leaving (one supposes) Edmund Bertram at hand. How convenient! Mary M. Threapleton, who provides the introduction to this edition, also lent her scholarly expertise to contemporary editions of Charlotte Brontë's *Jane Eyre* and Mary Shelley's *Frankenstein*.

ART: DODIE MASTERMAN

EVERYMAN LIBRARY

Sometimes the simplest covers can be the most (cost) effective. The illustration for this 1963 paperback edition of *Mansfield Park* evokes the feel of the novel, and the monochromatic motif saves the publisher, J. M. Dent & Sons, from ponying up for a more expensive four-color printing process. Here we have Fanny Price in her sanctum sanctorum, the East Room, formerly the schoolroom, where she sits sadly by candlelight. Perhaps she is avoiding the rehearsals of "Lovers' Vows," about which Mary Crawford and Edmund Bertram are more enthusiastic than they like to pretend, but she cannot help but think about them.

Her plants, her books . . . her writing-desk, and her works of charity and ingenuity, were all within her reach.

PAN CLASSICS

Novels of the late 1960s and early 1970s that were aimed at teenage girls typically featured a stylized portrait of the heroine on the cover, and these Pan Classics from Pan Books are no exception. On the *Northanger Abbey* version of 1968, Catherine Morland becomes a plucky girl hero in her own right, complete with cascading sixties' tresses, a dress that looks more Gunne Sax than British Regency, and a suspiciously sleepy-eyed expression. Likewise for 1971's *Sense and Sensibility*—it seems that Marianne Dashwood has stumbled onto a stash of magic mushrooms in her woodland wanderings (and here Elinor thought her sister's passion was for dead leaves!). *Persuasion*'s Captain Wentworth appears to be alarmed by Anne Elliot's décolletage, or perhaps that she seems to have forgotten to wear her stays. Or it could be that this is a fever dream of the post-accident Louisa Musgrove, her brain still a little scrambled, in which she wanders around Bath without her undergarments and with a tree sprouting from her bonnet.

Pan Classics
Jane Austen
Sense & Sensibility
Introduction and Notes by Dr. W.A. Craik

Pan Classics
Jane Austen
Persuasion
Introduction and Notes by Dr. W. A. Craik

MAGNUM EASY EYE LARGER TYPE FOR EASY READING

13-437/60¢

PERSUASION

JANE AUSTEN

COMPLETE AND UNABRIDGED

ART: JULIO FREIRE

14-607/75¢

PRIDE AND PREJUDICE

JANE AUSTEN

COMPLETE AND UNABRIDGED

ART: DICK KOHFIELD

ART: DICK KOHLFIELD

MAGNUM EASY EYE

These 1968 Lancer Books editions play pretty strictly within the bounds of sixties romance novel conventions, even if historically they take liberties with accuracy. The portrayal of the Napoleonic-era Royal Navy Captain Wentworth as the commander of a 1960s-era New England schooner is utterly egregious—he looks like he fell off an Old Spice bottle. Meanwhile, the back cover of *Northanger Abbey* bears the headline "Dark Shadows, Bright Humor," no doubt a none-too-subtle reference to the popular contemporary vampire soap opera *Dark Shadows*. There's a definite swoony angst to Catherine Morland's downcast doe eyes, and Henry Tilney—Austen's wittiest, most lighthearted hero—looks brooding, Byronic, rakish, and Rochesterish. As for *Pride and Prejudice*, once more unto the Brontë: the illustrator seems to have drawn the scene in which Jane Eyre first encounters Mr. Rochester and his dog rather than anything from *Pride and Prejudice* (even Mr. Darcy doesn't glower that much, and we're fairly certain he never wore a red bow tie).

PAPERBACK LIBRARY

This 1965 edition of *Northanger Abbey* is infamous in Janeite circles. Austen's novel is a parody of the Gothic tales popular during her time (just as the *Scream* movies parody today's horror films), but either the designer didn't get the memo or, more likely, some publishing higher-up thought the book would be more marketable as a capital-G Gothic novel, full of horrors and suspense. Under the chilling declaration that "The terror of Northanger Abbey had no name, no shape—yet it menaced Catherine Morland in the dead of night!" the heroine is clearly a woman in danger (her bright-red manicure notwithstanding). In the background looms the glowering hero and his cowboy-style string tie. And in case you still weren't scared, quotations from the novel, carefully syncopated for maximum Gothic-ness of content, add to the frightening presentation. In its own way, the cover image is quite brilliant and superbly (if inadvertently) tongue-in-cheek. Jane Austen would have loved it.

A NORTON CRITICAL EDITION

Pride and Prejudice

JANE AUSTEN

EDITED BY DONALD J. GRAY

AN AUTHORITATIVE TEXT
BACKGROUNDS
REVIEWS AND ESSAYS IN CRITICISM

NORTON CRITICAL EDITION

Even in the swingin' sixties, some publishers endeavored to produce editions with a more serious purpose. This "critical edition" of *Pride and Prejudice,* published in 1969 by W. W. Norton, includes not only an "authoritative" version of the text but also R. W. Chapman's chronology of the plot and more than a dozen scholarly essays. The publishers have followed in a long line of scholarly presentations, that is, spare and staid. The cover bears only an anonymous black-and-white photo of a large modern house that could be anywhere.

Pride and Prejudice

A NORTON CRITICAL EDITION

The text reprinted in this Norton Critical Edition is the one established by R. W. Chapman and universally acknowledged as definitive. To arrive at the text, Chapman collated three early editions of the novel, two published in 1813 and the third in 1817; the text is almost entirely that of the first edition of 1813.

To enable study of Jane Austen's developing craftsmanship, the editor has included in the Backgrounds section three important pieces of her juvenile writing. He also presents important Austen letters on the writing of fiction and on love and courtship, two essays on the composition of the novel, and Henry Austen's biographical notice.

The present edition offers several 19th-century reviews of Jane Austen's work and a number of important 20th-century essays which elucidate the novel, place it in its historical moment, specify the ways of its author's craft, and enlarge our idea of the character and weight of the matters it addresses. The critics include A. C. Bradley, Reginald Farrer, Mary Lascelles, Samuel Kliger, Dorothy Van Ghent, Reuben A. Brower, Marvin Mudrick, Andrew H. Wright, Howard S. Babb, E. M. Halliday, and A. Walton Litz.

THE EDITOR

Donald J. Gray received his Ph.D. from Ohio State University and is professor of English at Indiana University. He is presently editor of *College English.* He has written extensively on Victorian subjects and is the editor of the Norton Critical Edition of *Alice in Wonderland.*

ISBN 0-393-09668-8

The back cover continues the academic approach, noting the editor's scholarly additions to the volume.

LAUREL-LEAF EDITIONS

This 1971 Dell edition of *Emma* doesn't go to extreme lengths to make the story seem more dramatic, but certainly there's an effort to make the book appeal to readers of angsty romance novels. Miss Woodhouse looks as though she has A Scheme in mind for the unfortunate gentleman standing behind her (okay, maybe it's not that far off, for Emma is certainly a schemer!). The period details are mostly correct, though some are more Regency England by way of the 1970s. Indeed, the era was witnessing a growth in the popularity of BBC serial dramas, and many books published at this time reflected a similar aesthetic.

A mind lively and at ease, can do with seeing nothing, and can see nothing that does not answer.

The 1980s and Onward

The eighties saw the beginning of a distinctive divide in the packaging of Jane Austen's work: the commercial, the collectible, and the classic. Commercial books were inexpensively produced for mass-market readership, and their covers typically featured an original illustration of scenes or characters from the book. Collectible books were costlier to produce and designed as heirlooms, usually in a hardcover format. Classic editions, although not relegated exclusively to the realm of Austen scholarship, were nevertheless conceived with more "serious" readers in mind. The design struck a balance between the other two categories—cheap enough to use for everyday reading (or a college course), but elegant enough to please the discriminating Janeite.

Likewise, the cover designs tend to follow the same paradigm: the more commercial the package, the more literal the art. Scholarly editions might have a single thematic object or vignette; a more earnest edition might feature a period portrait of a young lady to suggest, but not necessarily illustrate, the book's heroine; and a mass-market edition could display a distinct depiction of a specific scene or character. Visually, this spectrum communicates different levels of accessibility. Depending on your edition, Austen's story is either as obvious as an illustration or as open to interpretation as a symbolic element of decoration. Here is a selection of these more recent trends.

PENGUIN ENGLISH LIBRARY EDITIONS

The Penguin English Library was first printed in the 1970s. The publisher continued to produce good, inexpensive, attractive editions of Jane Austen's novels and many others into the next decade, including this 1982 version of *Northanger Abbey*. Rather than sensationalize, the covers focused on simple, era-appropriate beauty conveyed through historically accurate paintings. These editions are still widely available and make excellent reading copies for the general reader and the serious scholar alike. *Persuasion*'s cover from 1971 features Lyme Regis, the coastal town in West Dorset where one of the novel's pivotal scenes takes place.

The engraving of the stormy scene is based on a painting by J. M. W. Turner.

The young people were all wild to see Lyme. . . . it was only seventeen miles from Uppercross; though November, the weather was by no means bad; . . . and to Lyme they were to go—Charles, Mary, Anne, Henrietta, Louisa, and Captain Wentworth.

—*Persuasion*

SIGNET CLASSIC

This 1980 Signet Classic edition of *Northanger Abbey* features an unidentified cover painting of a suitably forbidding-looking abbey, surrounded by a moat, that perfectly represents the eponymous abbey that Catherine Morland wished to see. However, sometimes the search for an "authentic" painting goes a bit off the rails, as with this edition of *Pride and Prejudice* (*below*), for which the designer seems to have conflated Austen's Regency England with the later Victorian era, complete with voluminous fabric folds and pronounced bustles.

The Signet Classics imprint of softbound reprints was originally part of the New American Library of World Literature, an independent publisher founded in 1948.

GREENWICH HOUSE CLASSICS LIBRARY

Crown Publishers' "complete and unabridged" 1982 edition of *Pride and Prejudice* is an interesting beast—a cross between the scholarly and the popular. It includes an introduction by the highly regarded critic Tony Tanner, as well as elements that a "serious" scholar might scorn, such as the illustrations by Hugh Thomson and a dreamy impressionistic watercolor painting on the dust jacket that looks straight out of the world of the French artist Auguste Renoir.

Greenwich House Classics Library

These are the finest editions available, with complete, authoritative texts, scholarly notes, introductions, and illustrations. Other titles in the series include:

The Adventures of Huckleberry Finn by Mark Twain. Edited with an introduction by Peter Coveney, with drawings by E.W. Kemble, the original illustrator. Huck and Jim's voyage down the Mississippi is the great American classic tale of boyhood adventure by the master wit and storyteller.

Madame Bovary by Gustave Flaubert, translated by Alan Russell and illustrated with etchings by Albert Fourié. One of the great creations of modern literature, Emma Bovary is the bored wife of a provincial doctor, whose desires and illusions are inevitably shattered when reality catches up with her.

The Odyssey translated by E.V. Rieu, with illustrations by John Flaxman. A superb modern translation of Homer's epic poem—the greatest adventure story of all time—recounting the experiences of Odysseus during his return from the Trojan War.

Robinson Crusoe by Daniel Defoe. Edited with an introduction by Angus Ross, with illustrations by J. D. Watson. The classic, engrossing account of shipwreck and survival on a desert island, by a master of narrative realism.

A Tale of Two Cities by Charles Dickens. Edited with an introduction by George Woodcock, with illustrations by Hablot L. Browne ("Phiz") and others. This moving and exciting tale of insurrection and renunciation set within the turmoil of the French Revolution is one of Dickens' best and most popular novels.

ISBN 0-517-385899

Crown was one of several publishers to reprint classics in uniform editions during the early 1980s.

PENGUIN CLASSICS (1980s)

In the mid-1980s, Penguin redesigned its Classics line, and in the 1990s it expanded the books' trim to a larger paperback size. The painting reproduced on the *Northanger Abbey* cover is of a gentleman showing some ladies around the gardens of a grand house, rather as General Tilney led Catherine Morland around the abbey. Poor Catherine wanted to see the Gothic details, like nuns' cells and dungeons, but the general insisted on sharing views of only the gardens and working areas. The painting is certainly bucolic, but probably rather dull to a romantically minded seventeen-year-old. The cover artwork shown on the circa-1985 edition of *Emma* is a detail from the portrait of Marcia B. Fox painted by the English artist Sir William Beechey (1753–1839). This same painting appears slightly "altered" on a 2009 cover of *Pride and Prejudice* (see page 151).

Regency-era portraits are a safe choice for the covers of Austen's novels.

ART: SIR WILLIAM BEECHEY, "MARCIA FOX"

ART: GEORGE SHEPHERD, DETAIL FROM "THE GARDENS AT BATTLESDEN HOUSE, BEDFORDSHIRE"

ART: ROBIN JACQUES

ZODIAC PRESS

This sturdy 1988 hardback from the Chatto & Windus imprint of Random House was designed for library use, and it is anything but Gothic. No sinister lurking men or dramatic cracks of lightning here: just a reassuring, familiar vignette with a storybook simplicity. The charming, if not quite period-correct, cover illustration by Robin Jacques makes the book feel friendly and approachable, perfect for tempting first-time Austen readers to pluck it off a library shelf.

Catherine's expectation of pleasure from her visit in Milsom Street were so very high that disappointment was inevitable . . .

BANTAM CLASSICS

Several publishers have determinedly kept mass-market paperback editions of Austen's novels as part of their line, changing the covers every so often to appeal to a new audience—many times without even resetting the text or adding new editorial content. Bantam Classics is one of those lines. Begun in 1958, the series encompasses the greats of world literature. This 1989 copy of *Northanger Abbey* is of its time—plain cover, sans-serif font, period painting set within a clean oval against a monochrome background. It's a lovely but unremarkable edition, the copy that one "inadvertently" leaves at the coffee shop in the hopes that some lucky person will discover the authoress for the first time.

But when a young lady is to be a heroine, the perverseness of forty surrounding families cannot prevent her. Something must and will happen to throw a hero in her way.

ART: GEORGE ENGLEHEART, "UNKNOWN WOMAN"

OXFORD ILLUSTRATED

The classics do endure: R. W. Chapman's edition of the *Oxford Illustrated Jane Austen* is still in print (page 37), with only slight changes to the notes and appendixes by other editors. This dust jacket dates from 1988 and features a bright blue-and-yellow design that is eye-catching on a bookshelf. The floral patterned frame recalls a Laura Ashley print, and the simple silhouette of Austen's profile is recognizable to fans and amateurs alike. The *Oxford Illustrated Jane Austen* novels are sold as a matched set of six. As noted on the back cover of this edition, each of the four early novels takes up its own volume, *Persuasion* and *Northanger Abbey* are paired together, and the *Minor Works*, including Austen's juvenile writing, unfinished works, and other ephemera, round out the collection. Unlike earlier books, the illustrations are not drawings depicting scenes in the novels, which Chapman found twee and unscholarly. Rather, they are fashion plates and prints showing details of architecture and everyday items such as carriages that date from the period in which the novels were written.

VIRAGO CLASSICS

Founded in 1973, Virago Press exists to publish and promote works by women authors, which means that Austen's books fit the company's list perfectly. This 1989 copy of *Mansfield Park* has a pretty period fashion-plate on the cover—a perfect representation of Mary Crawford, in her billowy dress and oversized hat.

Mary Crawford was remarkably pretty; Henry, though not handsome, had air and countenance; the manners of both were lively and pleasant, and Mrs. Grant immediately gave them credit for everything else. She was delighted with each, but Mary was her dearest object; and having never been able to glory in beauty of her own, she thoroughly enjoyed the power of being proud of her sister's.

PICTURING JANE

In person she was very attractive; her figure was rather tall and slender, her step light and firm, and her whole appearance expressive of health and animation. In complexion she was a clear brunette with a rich color; she had full round cheeks, with mouth and nose small and well formed, bright hazel eyes, and brown hair forming natural curls close round her face.

—J. E. AUSTEN-LEIGH, *A Memoir of Jane Austen*

WHAT DID JANE AUSTEN look like? We will likely never know for certain, but we can form a pretty good mind-portrait from reading her books and letters and the descriptions left by others. To help our imagination, we lean on a few images of the authoress that have come down to us from nearly her lifetime.

The only authenticated portrait of Jane Austen is a small pencil-and-watercolor sketch done by her sister Cassandra Austen. Many are dissatisfied with the image: the colors are faded, and the sitter does not look especially happy. On closer inspection, however, one sees that the details of the hair and eyes are very fine. Cassandra also painted another portrait of her sister, sitting down and facing away. It is only lacking in not showing Jane's face.

One of the best-known images is the silhouette that was found pasted into a copy of *Mansfield Park*, bearing the legend "*L'aimable Jane.*" It has long been accepted as a true likeness, though its provenance is unclear. Also well known is the so-called Rice painting. The story goes that one of Austen's cousins gave the painting to a neighbor, saying that it showed Jane and was done by the German painter Johann Zoffany. When the artwork was scrutinized in the twentieth century, it was determined not only that the portrait is by Ozias Humphry, but also that Austen would have been around thirty years old at the time it was painted, much older than the girl depicted.

Another charming, unauthenticated work appears in the "Friendship Book" of the Prince Regent's librarian, James Stanier Clarke. The tiny painting was made about the time that Clarke led Austen on a tour of the Prince Regent's London house. The woman's features match those described as Austen's: high cheekbones, high color, tall and slender. Surviving correspondence reveals that Clarke was rather taken with the authoress, increasing the possibility that he recorded her likeness as a keepsake.

Cassandra Austen's watercolor has inspired several spinoffs. The first is a painting by James Andrew that was commissioned by James Edward Austen-Leigh. It was converted into an engraving to be included with his "memoir" of his aunt published in 1870. The painting certainly sweetens Austen's expression, and perhaps contributes to the impression of many Janeites and scholars that the *Memoir* whitewashes its subject's personality. That image morphed into what is probably the best-known likeness, the "wedding ring" engraving that was used for a book of portraits of eminent persons. Austen has been expanded into a Victorian matron, complete with wedding ring. Despite the inaccuracies, she is respectfully placed as a woman of letters, surrounded by the accouterments of her profession.

A recent attempt at a likeness was made by the Jane Austen Centre in Bath. It hired a forensic portraitist who worked with existing images as well as descriptions of Austen's appearance. The result is a portrait of Jane Austen as she might have looked at the time she was publishing her novels (viewable online).

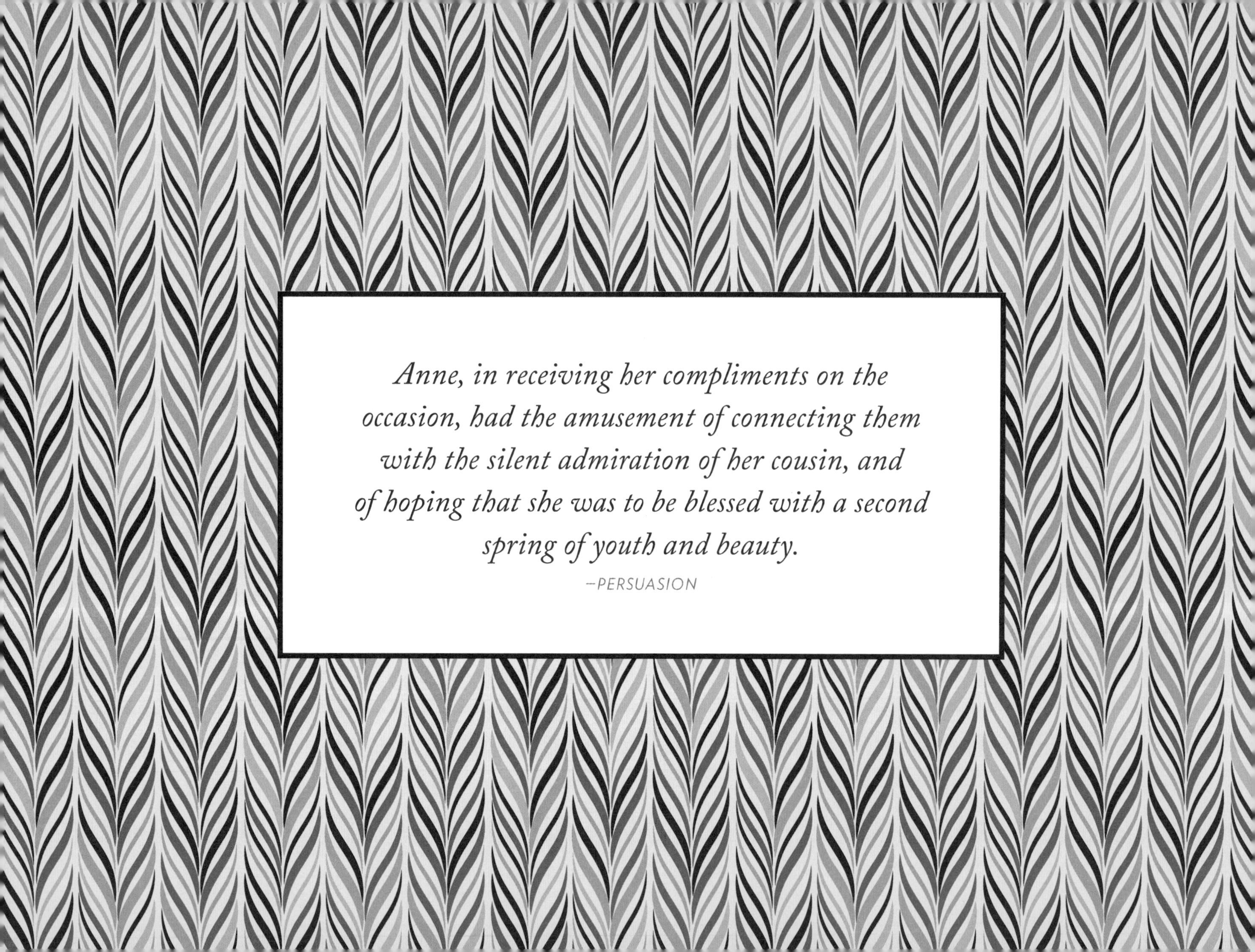

Anne, in receiving her compliments on the occasion, had the amusement of connecting them with the silent admiration of her cousin, and of hoping that she was to be blessed with a second spring of youth and beauty.

—PERSUASION

CHAPTER FOUR
A Second Spring

• 1990–2013 •

It was the splash heard 'round the world. Colin Firth as Mr. Darcy stripped to his shirtsleeves and dove into a pond on the grounds at Pemberley—well, it was his double who did the dive, but one does not wish to be a killjoy—and Jane Austen's work, until that time well-known but mostly quietly enjoyed, burst once more into public notice. Between the explosion of entertainment and cultural media, the Internet, and a spate of mostly excellent film adaptations of her novels, the 1990s saw an intense media spotlight fixed on all things Austen that continues unabated today.

Aside from film tie-in books (see Chapter Five), publishers continued to doggedly produce new editions of Austen's classics, in addition to rolling out her long-ignored early works and juvenilia. Increasingly, cover design and packaging came to reflect the different audiences for Austen's work. With a design similar to that of genre romance, inexpensive paperback editions with original cover illustrations continued to court casual readers. Sturdily bound hardcovers headed for the library shelves. Meanwhile, commemorative and collectible volumes encouraged artists to experiment and invent variations on the themes that Austen so deftly wove into her fiction.

With almost two centuries having passed since the first publications of her work, Austen and her novels had settled into the realm of history. The elegant "classic" editions produced in the nineties and beyond found a sizable audience of academics and scholarly readers eager for additional pages of notes and commentary on the life of this treasured author.

RIVERDALE CLASSICS

Speaking as a representative of Team Tilney—that is, fans of *Northanger Abbey*'s hero, Henry Tilney—this 1990 cover of the Riverdale Classics edition is amusing, especially the, shall we say, fortuitous positioning of the declaration "Complete and Unabridged." (No doubt Mr. Tilney was relieved.) Catherine, with her Glamazon smile and teased updo, looks rather older than seventeen, and Henry is inappropriately brooding under something of a Cro-Magnon brow. Perhaps this image is meant to show Mr. and Mrs. Tilney after ten years of marriage? Still happy, and still unabridged!

ART: CHLOE CHEESE

LONGMAN GROUP UK LTD.

The cover illustration of this 1991 edition of *Pride and Prejudice* appears to be based on a work by Rolinda Sharples (1793–1838), an English portrait painter and contemporary of Jane Austen. Sharples's 1817 painting *The Cloak-Room, Clifton Assembly Rooms* is relatively singular, for few extant paintings from the Georgian era depict lively parties such as this. It is thus a perennially popular choice for books about Jane Austen and her time. Eagle-eyed Janeites will recognize it gracing the fronts of several works of Austen scholarship, including *A Portrait of Jane Austen* by David Cecil and *Jane Austen: The World of Her Novels* by Deirdre Le Faye, as well as the cover of the Wordsworth Edition of *Persuasion* shown on page 85.

ELIZABETH BENNET: *"Did not you think, Mr. Darcy, that I expressed myself uncommonly well just now, when I was teazing Colonel Forster to give us a ball at Meryton?"*

MR. DARCY: *"With great energy;—but it is a subject which always makes a lady energetic."*

SONO NIS PRESS

This silly little story, written when Jane Austen was twelve years old, has been charmingly illustrated by the Austen scholar Juliet McMaster in a 1993 edition meant for children. For the serious budding Janeite, *The Beautifull Cassandra*—rather than the rewritten juvenile adaptations of the novels (such as those on pages 156–157)—is the preferred introduction to her oeuvre. In an afterword, McMaster explains that she chose a mouse to represent the title character because the story reminded her of Beatrix Potter, sparking the idea of a tale populated by animal characters.

When Cassandra had attained her 16th year, she was lovely & amiable, & chancing to fall in love with an elegant Bonnet her Mother had just compleated, bespoke by the Countess of —, she placed it on her gentle Head & walked from her Mother's shop to make her Fortune.

ART: ILLUSTRATION, JULIET MCMASTER; PORTRAIT, CASSANDRA AUSTEN

DESIGN: ROBBIN GOURLEY

ALGONQUIN BOOKS

JUVENILIA PRESS HISTORY OF ENGLAND

When she was sixteen years old, Jane Austen wrote a parody of the scholarly history books she read as a schoolgirl. Her sister Cassandra contributed amusing watercolor illustrations of the characters depicted in the history. The original manuscript can be viewed (behind glass) at the British Library and is well worth a visit. Fortunately, Janeites everywhere can enjoy facsimile editions, such as this 1993 be-ribboned version from the U.S. publisher Algonquin Books as well as the more restrained Australian version from 2009 (*below*).

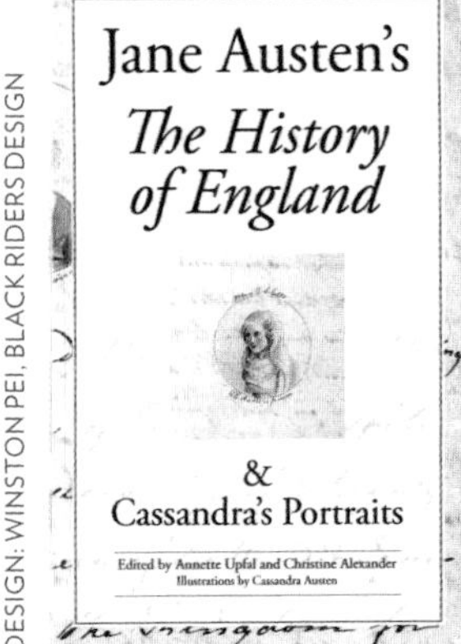

DESIGN: WINSTON PEI, BLACK RIDERS DESIGN

Like the volume shown at left, this Juvenilia Press edition also reproduces Cassandra Austen's illustrations.

OXFORD WORLD'S CLASSICS

Several editions of Jane Austen's early work were published in the 1990s, including *Catharine*, a work of juvenilia whose titular heroine had the misfortune, "as many heroines have had before her, of losing her parents when she was very young." It's hard to say exactly what spurred this new wave of interest in the fringes of Austen's work; perhaps publishers simply wanted to expand their horizons (and their market share) beyond the Big Six novels. The Oxford World's Classics 1993 edition of *Catharine and Other Writings* (*center*) includes most of Austen's juvenile works. This 2003 edition of *Northanger Abbey* (*right*) presents unfinished works and other stories that Austen wrote as an adult.

ART: R. ACKERMANN, DETAIL OF "NEWSTEAD ABBEY" FROM "REPOSITORY OF ARTS"

ART: JEAN-BAPTISTE FRANÇOIS DESORIA, "PORTRAIT OF CONSTANCE P."

ART: FREDERICK SAY, DETAIL FROM "ROBERT ROBINSON AND HIS FAMILY"

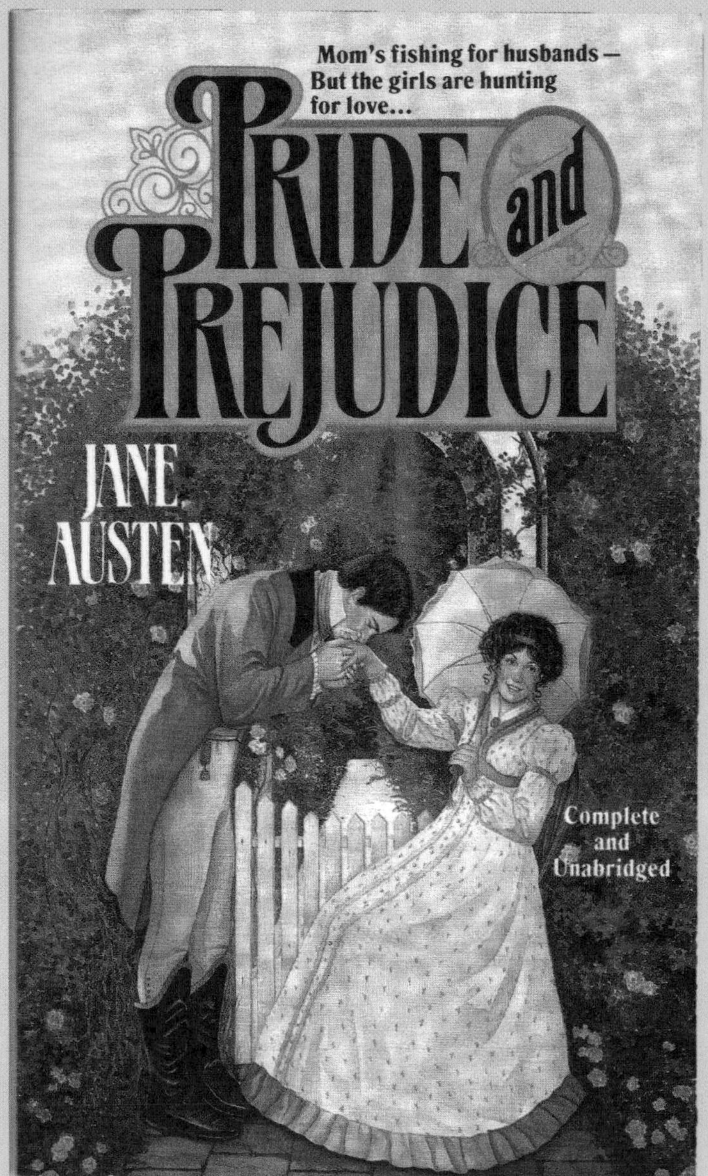
Mom's fishing for husbands—
But the girls are hunting
for love…
PRIDE and PREJUDICE
JANE AUSTEN
Complete
and
Unabridged

JANE AUSTEN
Sense and Sensibility
TOR
54312-2 $2.99 (CAN $3.99)
Two sisters.
Two romances.
A tragic tale
of love and deceit…

ART: WILLIAM MAUGHAN; DESIGN: JOE CURCIO

TOR MASS-MARKET EDITIONS

The Tor editions of Tom Doherty Associates are wonderful examples of the more commercial look that the packaging of Austen's work took in the 1990s. They most resemble the cover images of period romance novels. *Pride and Prejudice*, from 1994, features a swooping rococo title and a frizzy wreath of rosebushes, beneath which Mr. Darcy kisses Elizabeth's hand (and then probably serenades her with a crooned rendition of "Purple Rain"). The tagline may be the best-ever bad summary of the novel's plot, though the whole field-and-stream metaphor isn't too unsuited to Mrs. Bennet's rather predatory behavior. The 1995 cover of *Sense and Sensibility* is likewise a bit tone deaf. Perhaps these two young women are the rather uncouth Anne and Lucy Steele, for the Dashwood sisters surely wouldn't gossip so carelessly beneath a parasol that appears to be melting. In the hyperrealistic 1999 illustration of *Persuasion*, Captain Wentworth pays special attention to the Musgrove sisters, either for their abundance of exposed bosom or for their carefully matched shawl-and-gown combo. Meanwhile, poor Anne Elliot bites her hand in horror . . . perhaps because the Bath Abbey peeking through the window bears a striking resemblance to the Alamo.

READER'S DIGEST

Reader's Digest produced this edition in 1994 as part of a series called "The World's Best Reading" (a designation we can get behind!). The series is a mail-order book club that republishes classic works. All of Austen's novels have appeared, with *Pride and Prejudice* published twice, in 1984 and 2011. It's quite an attractive hardback edition, with illustrations by C. E. Brock and Joan Hassall reprinted from earlier editions.

It encourages me to depend on the same share of general good opinion which Emma's predecessors have experienced, and to believe that I have not yet, as almost every writer of fancy does sooner or later, overwritten myself.

Letter from JANE AUSTEN to the Countess of Morley
dated December 31, 1815

ART: JOAN HASSALL

ART: HENRY FUSELI, "THE NIGHTMARE"

SIGNET CLASSIC

In this 1995 offering from Penguin Books, "Two Gothic Classics by Women" share the bill: Austen's satirical Gothic romp accompanies one of the very novels it was meant to poke fun at, *The Italian* by Anne Radcliffe. Mysterious occurrences, romantic prose, and virtuous heroines were the hallmarks of Radcliffe's work, so it's no surprise that Austen chose that author's *Mysteries of Udolpho* as Catherine Morland's favorite. The painting chosen for cover—Henry Fuseli's *Nightmare*—was first exhibited in 1782 at the Royal Academy of London, where its lurid chiaroscuro rendering of a woman trapped in a swoon by an otherworldly beast caused a scandal among buttoned-up art lovers, a detail that Miss Morland would no doubt appreciate.

CATHERINE: *"No, indeed, I should not. I do not pretend to say that I was not very much pleased with him; but while I have Udolpho to read, I feel as if nobody could make me miserable."*

WORDSWORTH CLASSICS

These handsome hardback editions of 1995 come from Wordsworth, a U.K. publisher that originally specialized in affordable £1 paperback copies of classic books. These editions, designed by Robert Mathias, are particularly handsome. For the covers of *Northanger Abbey* and *Mansfield Park*, evocative paintings representing the titles' great houses were chosen. For *Persuasion*, the publisher opted for a well-known 1817 painting by Rolinda Sharples, *The Cloakroom, Clifton Assembly Rooms*, which depicts a scene from a society gathering of Austen's time period.

ART: APELY PRIOR; DESIGN: ROBERT MATHIAS

ART: THORP PERROW, "NEAR SNAPE, YORKSHIRE"; DESIGN: ROBERT MATHIAS

ART: ROLINDA SHARPLES, 'THE CLOAKROOM, CLIFTON ASSEMBLY ROOMS'; DESIGN: ROBERT MATHIAS

ORION BOOKS LTD.

Published in 1996, this tiny booklet, about half the size of a paperback, contains only Austen's unfinished short story *Catharine*. It's a quick read and presents an exercise in either frustration or imagination, for one can't help but wonder where Austen might have taken the story. Written when Austen was sixteen, it anticipates her later novels with its plot about a young lady entering society.

To Miss Austen Madam
Encouraged by your warm patronage of The beautiful Cassandra, *and* The History of England, *which through your generous support, have obtained a place in every library in the Kingdom, and run through threescore Editions, I take the liberty of begging the same Exertions in favour of the following Novel, which I humbly flatter myself, possesses Merit beyond any already published, or any that will ever in future appear, except such as may proceed from the pen of*
Your Most Grateful Humble Servt
The Author
Steventon August 1792

—DEDICATION TO *CATHARINE, OR THE BOWER*

JANE AUSTEN
CATHARINE

ART: BONNOT/IMAGE BANK

ART: WILLIAM BLAKE, "PORTRAIT OF MRS. Q (MRS. HARRIET QUENTIN)"; DESIGN: JOHN M. ALVES

DOVER THRIFT EDITIONS

As the name suggests, Dover Thrift Editions are not fancy, but they make perfectly acceptable additions to the libraries of a general readership and are affordable to boot. The cover is usually attractive; at the lowest of low list prices (these sold for a mere $3.50), designers are restricted to free or inexpensive decoration. The choice of image on the 1999 edition of *Pride and Prejudice* is an interesting one: the painting is thought to be the work referenced in an 1813 letter from Jane Austen to her sister, telling her about an exhibition of paintings in London. Jane whimsically wrote that one of the paintings was of "Mrs. Bingley," the former Jane Bennet, one of the characters in the book: "Mrs Bingley's is exactly herself, size, shaped face, features & sweetness; there never was a greater likeness. She is dressed in a white gown, with green ornaments, which convinces me of what I had always supposed, that green was a favourite colour with her."

DESIGN: TERESA DELGADO

The bold floral print calls to mind the designs of English pre-Raphaelite artist William Morris.

SIGNET CLASSIC

The 1990s Signet Classic editions keep the design of their previous decade's predecessors (see page 64). The cover of *Mansfield Park* features an painting of an unidentified church that looks suspiciously like the one at Steventon, the Hampshire village in which Jane Austen grew up. Even if it is a different structure, it's certainly fitting for Austen's most serious novel about the effect of education on one's morality. The inset portrait on *Northanger Abbey* is of Miss Harriet Beechey, painted by Sir William Beechey, the same portraitist who painted Miss Marcia Fox (page 66).

The Classics were redesigned in the 2000s; the new covers featured oval inset images, as here.

ART: SIR WILLIAM BEECHEY, "MISS HARRIET BEECHEY"

DESIGN: MARYSARAH QUINN

NEW YORK PUBLIC LIBRARY COLLECTOR'S EDITION

The New York Public Library Collector's Edition of *Mansfield Park* was produced by Doubleday in 1997 as a fund-raiser for the library. The lovely hardback was apparently the only Austen novel produced for this purpose—an interesting choice, given that *Mansfield Park* isn't exactly her most popular work. Rather than illustrate characters or settings from the story, the cover features Austen's signature and a colorized version of the nineteenth-century engraving created from Cassandra Austen's famous portrait of her sister (see "Picturing Jane" sidebar, page 71).

THE MODERN LIBRARY CLASSICS

Random House publishes large-format paperbacks, with the volumes shown here dating from 1996 and 2001. A cover illustration by Hugh Thomson was used for *Pride and Prejudice*, and period portraits grace the other novels. The quotes by famous authors—set within the white bar holding the title—are an especially thoughtful touch, helping to underscore Austen's influence on those in her profession. As implied by the clean, classic design and use of fine paintings as illustration, these are excellent student editions for the more serious reader or collector. They also contain an introduction by respected writers as well as notes and extra information. Together, the books make a lovely matched set.

ART: HUGH THOMSON; DESIGN: GABRIELLE BORDWIN

ART: THOMAS SULLY, "THE MCEVEN SISTERS"; DESIGN: GABRIELLE BORDWIN

ART: THOMAS SULLY, "PORTRAIT OF MARGARET DOUGLAS"; DESIGN: GABRIELLE BORDWIN

ART: THOMAS BENJAMIN-KENNINGTON, "FORBIDDEN FRUIT"; DESIGN: GABRIELLE BORDWIN

ROMANCE CLASSICS

This edition was published by Trident Press International in 2001. It is composed of tiny text, and the negative image of (one supposes) Miss Woodhouse can come across as unsettling. However, the period fashion plate on the cover is both attractive and proper. (For more on Regency fashions, see "Fashion Plate," page 185.)

To Emma's query, reprinted on the back cover, Mr. Knightley replies: "Not your vain spirit, but your serious spirit. If one leads you wrong, I am sure the other tells you of it."

HEADLINE REVIEW

Headline Review put out this set of Austen's novels in 2006, intended for a general audience. The publisher set up a microsite for the set (since vanished from the Internet) and included reading group questions, though little other supplementary material was provided. The covers were described in press releases as designed to attract readers who would not normally choose Jane Austen as their reading material. Despite a lot of discussion and indignant commentary in the press and on blogs, it's hard to see the delicate colors and simple design as anything but lovely.

"I can listen no longer in silence. I must speak to you by such means as are within my reach. You pierce my soul. I am half agony, half hope."

EVERYMAN

The Everyman Library has its roots in the late-nineteenth-century editions illustrated by Charles Brock, which were published by J. M. Dent & Co., and the even earlier editions with introductions by the critic R. Brimley Johnson. These editions—a 1997 *Sense and Sensibility* from J. M. Dent and a 1992 *Persuasion* from Alfred A. Knopf—contain supplementary materials meant for students and Janeites alike. The cover of *Sense and Sensibility* reproduces a period fashion plate of a riding habit. Is that Willoughby lurking in the background, bringing Queen Mab, the horse he bought for Marianne Dashwood? *Persuasion* features the so-called Rice Portrait, which may or may not portray Jane Austen as a tween with a pixie haircut. Though long attributed to the German-born artist Johann Zoffany, the painting was later identified by scholars as a work by the English portraitist Ozias Humphry (see "Picturing Jane" sidebar, page 71).

Scholars to this day debate over whether the girl in this painting is Jane Austen.

ART: N. HEIDELOFF, "RIDING DRESS" FROM "GALLERY OF FASHION"

ENRICHED
CLASSIC

PRIDE AND PREJUDICE

JANE AUSTEN

Includes detailed explanatory notes,
an overview of key themes, and more

ART: MARC BURCKHARDT

ENRICHED CLASSIC

Like many publishers, including Everyman Library (*opposite*), Pocket Books follows a standard cover formula that presents a variation on the grid revolutionized by Penguin in the 1930s. An image takes up the upper two-thirds, with the author's name and title, separated by a simple rule, in a bold color band below. The name of the series (or, often, the publisher or imprint) occupies a prominent position between the two. The effect is meant to catch the eye and convey a serious study of classic literature. Here, the reproduction of a painting once again presents us with a symbolic peacock, perhaps an homage to Hugh Thomson's iconic 1890s edition (page 26).

He looked for a moment at Elizabeth, till catching her eye, he withdrew his own and coldly said, "She is tolerable; but not handsome enough to tempt me."

TOBY CLASSICS

The popularity of illustrated covers likely prompted the Toby Press, an Israeli English-language publisher, to choose this arresting close-up of a wood engraving for its 2001 version of *Pride and Prejudice*. This volume fits into the publisher's mission to provide "quality editions of enduring classics at low prices." Other authors reprinted in the line of hardbacks offered "under $10" include Charles Dickens and Nathaniel Hawthorne.

"Had I been in love, I could not have been more wretchedly blind. But vanity, not love, has been my folly."

ART: CASSANDRA AUSTEN, "PORTRAIT OF JANE AUSTEN"

CAMBRIDGE EDITION

Cambridge University Press went all-out on this 2006 set of Austen's novels, declaring their intention to replace the *Oxford Illustrated Jane Austen* as the definitive edition for scholars and students. They have certainly lived up to their intention. Each volume includes not only a new edition of the text based on collations of early editions but also an exhaustive amount of notes, essays, and supplementary materials. Also provided is an additional volume, *Jane Austen in Context*, that includes yet more essays about the history and culture of the period in which the novels are set. On their release, the textbook cost of these books was prohibitively expensive for many fans, but the price has since dropped, and a less expensive paperback version is now available. The cover illustration is as definitive as the text: Cassandra Austen's watercolor portrait of her sister, the only image of Austen known to have been done during her lifetime.

BROADVIEW PRESS LTD.

The Canadian publisher Broadview Press publishes truly excellent editions of Austen's novels, with some of the best supplementary material available. Like all their editions of nineteenth-century classics, this 2001 copy of *Sense and Sensibility* features a cover that reproduces a Victorian-era photograph. A period portrait may offer a rosy imagining of a heroine's face. This one, however, might provide too much detail. Surely lovely Marianne and sensible Elinor weren't as tight-lipped as these prim and dour maidens, with their thousand-yard stares and hair plastered over their ears. How is Willoughby supposed to clip a lock?

ART: PHOTOGRAPHER UNKNOWN, "EMILY AND FRANCES ANNA SAVAGE"

COLLECTOR'S LIBRARY

These sweet little books are delightful throwbacks to early editions of Austen's work, made tiny to be discreetly tucked away in a pocket. Sized a little smaller than 6 by 4 inches, they remind one of a prayer book or other volume intended for portable, personal reflection. Published by CRW Publishing in 2004, this book includes reproductions of Hugh Thomson's nineteenth-century illustrations (page 26).

"My idea of good company, Mr. Elliot, is the company of clever, well-informed people, who have a great deal of conversation; that is what I call good company."

ROBERT FREDERICKS LTD.

The Fredericks Illustrated set of the novels features a selection of the watercolor paintings by C. E. Brock from the early twentieth-century Dent editions, along with some of the Hugh Thomson pen-and-ink drawings from the late-nineteenth-century George Allen and Macmillan editions. The front and back cover of this 2005 edition of *Pride and Prejudice* includes the Brock painting of Mr. Darcy's second—successful—proposal of marriage to Elizabeth Bennet. Sort of a spoiler, one might think.

Elizabeth . . . immediately, though not very fluently, gave him to understand that her sentiments had undergone so material a change . . . as to make her receive with gratitude and pleasure his present assurances.

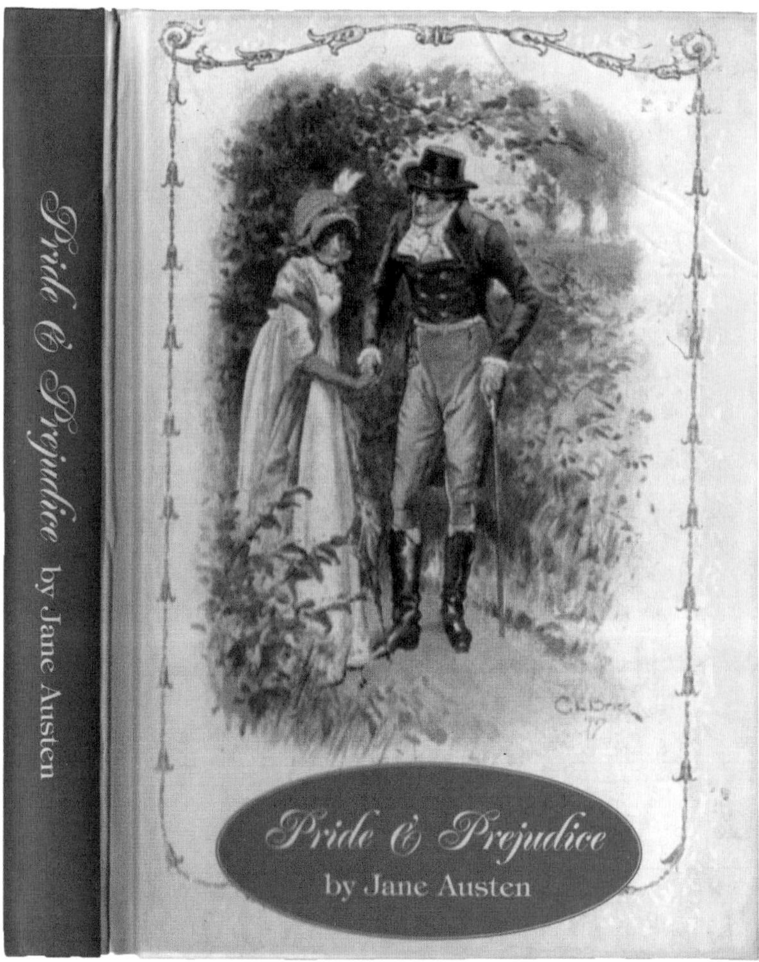

ART: C. E. BROCK

ART: NIROOT PUTTAPIPAT

FOLIO SOCIETY

The Folio Society publishes luxurious collectible editions of classic novels, and this 2007 edition of *Emma* is an excellent example. The binding is made to look like a period half-calf rebinding, complete with a patterned background and an inset medallion containing an ink-and-wash painting, presumably of the title character. The effect is of a treasured family portrait hanging on a wallpapered wall.

RED CLASSICS

In 2006, a few years into the new millennium, Penguin published a new Austen set called the Red Classics. All feature delightful, minimalist cover illustrations by Kazuko Nomoto, such as the one of Anne Elliot and Captain Wentworth clasping hands on the cover of *Persuasion*. The editions were also sold bundled in a box set of "The Great Novels of Jane Austen," which sounds perfectly splendid except only five novels were included. Jane Austen, as we all know, wrote *six* novels, all of them great. So which was missing? *Northanger Abbey*.

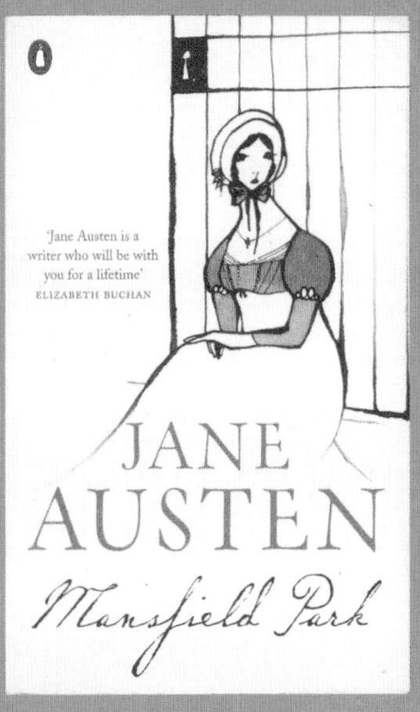

FOR ALL: ART BY KAZUKO NOMOTO. DESIGN BY CLARE SKEATS

SCHOLASTIC CLASSICS

As with many of the chunkier and sturdier hardback editions, this solid, large 2007 hardcover, with its pretty painting and cloth binding, appears to be intended for a school library. The foreword was written by Katherine Paterson, author of the popular children's book *Bridge to Terabithia*.

ELIZABETH BENNET: *"I am not a great reader, and I have pleasure in many things."*

ART: WILLIAM KAY BLACKLOCK, "A QUIET READ"

ART: JOHANN HEINRICH MUNTZ, "VIEW OF THE VYNE FROM THE NORTHWEST"; DESIGN: PATRICE KAPLAN

BARNES & NOBLE SIGNATURE EDITIONS

American bookseller Barnes and Noble has published a variety of editions of Austen's novels and other public domain classics, with packaging aimed at students, collectors, and fans rather than casual readers. This 2012 hardback is particularly handsome. Its dust jacket displays a picturesque painting called *View of the Vyne*. The Vyne was a house in the Hampshire neighborhood where Jane Austen grew up, making it a particularly apt choice.

But whatever may be the beauties or defects of the surrounding scenery . . . this was the cradle of her genius. These were the first objects which inspired her young heart with a sense of the beauties of nature.

—J. E. AUSTEN-LEIGH, *A Memoir of Jane Austen*

TOWNSEND LIBRARY EDITION

The Townsend Library editions are meant for the educational market. The cover illustration by Hal Taylor on this 2007 volume is a graphic representation of Elizabeth and Darcy—an interesting mix of period details and modern style. Certain details ring a little false, such as that rose in Miss Bennet's decolletage and her black ribbon choker. Nevertheless, the resulting image is undeniably eye-catching, and the overlapping figures and sideways glances capture the novel's story nicely.

"My mind was more agreeably engaged. I have been meditating on the very great pleasure which a pair of fine eyes in the face of a pretty woman can bestow."

ART: HAL TAYLOR

HERITAGE CLASSICS

It is hard to believe that Heritage published this book in 2007, given its romantic clinch cover that looks more like a romance novel from a few decades earlier. Is that Mr. Darcy in dishabille, clasping Elizabeth Bennet in his manly arms as she looks around wildly for Lady Catherine de Bourgh, come to interrupt the encroaching Miss Bennet from practicing her arts and allurements on her nephew? Or perhaps it shows Mr. Wickham trying to seduce young Georgiana Darcy? (It is likely not Mr. Wickham seducing Lydia Bennet—she wouldn't have tried to get away.) The illustration is delightfully, amusingly out of place for any Jane Austen novel, yet its campy mood reflects a popular trend in book covers that will never go out of style.

INSIGHT EDITION

This 2007 edition, a product of the Christian publisher Bethany House, includes annotations and commentary for readers seeking, yes, insight, into themes of Christian faith in Jane Austen's work. The idea of a religious take on a secular love story might seem out of place, but Austen was deeply religious and may well have appreciated this approach. (The biographical blurb refers to "Jane Austen, a clergyman's daughter.") More controversial than the additional content, however, is the cover, whose soft focus and verdant background engendered its share of Internet snark for resembling so-called bonnet porn, those chaste novels about the romantic and spiritual tribulations of Amish and Mennonite couples.

Miss Austen has the merit (in our judgment most essential) of being evidently a Christian writer: a merit which is much enhanced . . . by her religion being not at all obtrusive.

—RICHARD WHATELY, in an unsigned review, quoted in J. E. Austen-Leigh, *A Memoir of Jane Austen*

ART: JEAN-PAUL TIBBLES

PUFFIN CLASSICS

Penguin's Puffin Classics line has been publishing books for juvenile readers for decades, and it is not surprising that they would rejacket Jane Austen in a package meant to appeal to teens. This 1996 edition of *Sense and Sensibility* features a lovely painting of the Dashwood sisters by Jean-Paul Tibbles that clearly shows the ladies' youth, something one would think would be attractive to its audience.

ART: © SHUTTERSTOCK; DESIGN: JANA SINGER

The series' classic look later underwent an overhaul, as seen in the covers shown on the back of this 2011 *Emma*.

HESPERUS PRESS

Austen's last, unfinished work, *Sanditon* is a novel centered on a small seaside resort of the same name and the families that populate it. Austen had originally titled it "The Brothers" when she began writing in January 1817, abandoning the project only three months later; the new title was bestowed by her family after her death. Charlotte Heywood, the brothers Parker, and the rest of Sanditon have long been a tempting jumping-off point for Janeites to "complete" the work, but this edition reproduces only Austen's eleven chapters. As for the chicken cover on this 2009 edition, well, let's call it whimsical.

"I hope you will eat some of this toast," said he. "I reckon myself a very good toaster. I never burn my toasts, I never put them too near the fire at first. And yet, you see, there is not a corner but what is well browned. I hope you like dry toast."

—Sandition

VINTAGE CLASSIC EDITIONS

In accordance with its name, the Vintage Classic editions of Random House have always had an attractive presentation that's fresh and modern without pandering to potential readers. The versions published in the United Kingdom feature graphic cover design by Birgit Amadori. *Sense and Sensibility* elegantly establishes the sisterly dynamic of the Dashwoods: though similarly posed, they look in different directions but their hearts are always close. Amadori's design for *Persuasion*, showing Anne Elliot gazing at a ship in a bottle, is the perfect metaphor for Anne's long wait for her sailor to return.

For its U.S. customers, Vintage used period fashion plates to illustrate the covers. The one used for *Mansfield Park* is an excellent choice. Is that Fanny Price giving Mary Crawford the side-eye?

ART: BIRGIT AMADORI

ART: BIRGIT AMADORI

Jane Austen

MANSFIELD PARK

ART: N. HEIDELOFF, "FASHION PLATE" FROM "GALLERY OF FASHION"; DESIGN: MEGAN WILSON

OXFORD WORLD'S CLASSICS

In the 2000s, Oxford University Press redesigned its Oxford World's Classics editions with a minimalist design incorporating a period painting. In this 2008 example for *Mansfield Park*, a demure-looking young lady perfectly represents the shy and retiring Fanny Price. The main advantage of these books is that they contain much of the same content as the *Oxford Illustrated Jane Austen*, including R. W. Chapman's notes on the text and other supplemental material, but are offered at a relatively inexpensive price.

Jane Austen was successful in everything she attempted with her fingers. . . . Her needlework both plain and ornamental was excellent and might almost have put a sewing machine to shame.

—J. E. AUSTEN-LEIGH, *A Memoir of Jane Austen*

ART: MARIA SPILSBURY, DETAIL FROM "GROUP PORTRAIT AT A DRAWING ROOM TABLE"

DK ILLUSTRATED CLASSICS

The British publisher Dorling-Kindersley is best known for its photo-illustrated reference books, an approach the company lends to enrich the world of Austen's fiction with visual additions right on the page. This softcover edition from 2008 is printed on glossy magazine-like paper, with color photographs of period homes, carriages, and other details throughout.

The back cover design imitates the front, with its four-square layout of colored blocks containing illustrative details and text.

SIGNET CLASSICS

A new millennium brought a total design overhaul for the previously traditional Signet editions (pages 64, 83, and 88). A lively and whimsical design, bright backgrounds, and a playful font script refresh and revitalize the imprint, transforming its oil-portrait and landscape-painting past into an eye-catching package reminiscent of chick lit, still a booming subgenre. The candlestick serves as a logical enough icon for *Northanger Abbey*, but one does wonder at what point a rowboat would feature in *Persuasion* . . .

As is common in reprinted editions, these include afterwords by well-known novelists and writers.

ART: CASSANDRA CHOUINARD; DESIGN: LAURA MCDONALD

JANE AUSTEN BICENTENARY LIBRARY EDITION

The Janeite world happily took to celebrating the two hundredth anniversary of the publication of Austen's novels, marking the event with many new editions. This 2011 example is charmingly illustrated by Cassandra Chouinard, including the cover illustration of Marianne Dashwood taking a walk and getting her stockings wet.

They gaily ascended the downs, rejoicing in their own penetration at every glimpse of blue sky.

ANCHOR BOOKS REVISED AND ANNOTATED EDITION

These Anchor Books annotated editions of Austen's novels have been extremely popular. Each has the book text printed on the left leaf and annotations on the right; the latter includes notes about historical context, excerpted material from the author's life and letters, definitions, and other critical analysis. Perhaps superfluous for a quick readthrough, such a wealth of information is wonderfully informative for the true Janeite. The cover illustration of this 2012 reprint of *Pride and Prejudice* reproduces a portrait of Jane Austen's niece Fanny Austen-Knight, painted by Cassandra Austen. It, too, is annotated—hence the little numbers. The notes to it are on the first page of the book.

Oh, dear Fanny! your mistake has been one that thousands of women fall into. He was the first young man who attached himself to you. That was the charm, and most powerful it is.

—JANE AUSTEN in a letter to her niece Fanny Knight dated November 18, 1814

ART: CASSANDRA AUSTEN, "FANNY AUSTEN-KNIGHT"; DESIGN: MEGAN WILSON

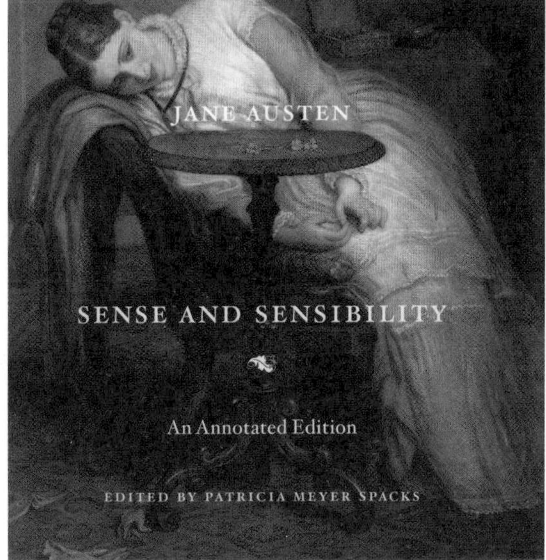

DESIGN: GRACIELA GALUP

HARVARD ANNOTATED EDITIONS

Here we have a scholarly set of each of Austen's novels published by the Belknap Press of Harvard University Press in celebration of the two hundredth anniversary of their first publication. These books are huge—oversize, lavishly illustrated coffee-table tomes unwieldy to read but beautiful to behold. They feature not only period paintings and earlier drawings from the novels but also annotations of both critical and cultural information. They're not the easiest to tote around, but Janeites have gone wild for them, understandably so.

HARPERTEEN

Janeites like to pass on their passion for their beloved author to younger generations. So it is to be earnestly hoped that this series by HarperCollins from 2009–11 has brought teenage fans of romance over to the Austen camp. Inspired by the stark red-and-black covers of the iconic *Twilight* series, the designs are so minimalist as to be (mostly) inoffensive. It's the taglines that are more difficult to accept: "The Love That Started It All" and "Love Is a Game" aren't technically wrong, but they aren't exactly right, either.

As the back cover directs: collect them all!

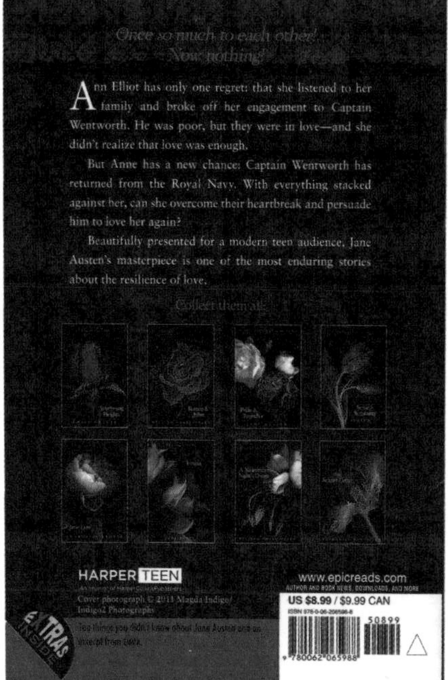

ART: MAGDA INDIGO/INDIGO2 PHOTOGRAPHY

BLOOMSBURY CLASSICS

In the wake of the 2005 film adaptation of *Pride and Prejudice*, the British publisher Bloomsbury came out with this newly packaged version in 2007, promising "hasty judgements and heartache, scandalous behaviour, and, finally, true love." Bright colors, a simple design, and a "Why you should read this" introduction by Meg Cabot, author of *The Princess Diaries*, make this an edition for the tween set. The back cover playfully insists that "you can really impress your mates (and teachers!) with all the juicy facts at the back of the book."

Small Press, Internet, and E-Book Editions

Change is constant in publishing as in life. Just as with the advent of lithography, paperbacks, and the commuter-reader in days gone by, the appearance and, now, dominance of the digital world have revolutionized the production and distribution of Jane Austen's works. Even as publishing technology becomes cheaper, faster, and easier, Austen's canon remains in the up-for-grabs public domain, making it easy for independent, digital, and print-on-demand presses to whip up their own versions. The resulting generation of editions is unlike any before: covers range from simple jpeg files attached to an e-book to well-intentioned but anachronistic photo spreads. The aesthetic of these covers is all over the place—much like the Internet itself.

LITERARY TOUCHSTONE CLASSICS

American educational publisher Prestwick House focuses on helping students "use English/Language Arts to become better readers and writers, learn to love literature, and succeed in the 21st century." Complete with vocabulary glossaries and "reading pointers" written and compiled by teachers, this 2005 *Pride and Prejudice* is meant for the U.S. junior and senior high school classroom. The cover resorts to the usual conceit: a modern photo showing characters in period clothing (though the choice of dress material—polyester—is certainly anachronistic), likely meant to appeal to the student audience. Still, one cannot imagine a better way to encourage young readers to appreciate the English language and literary canon than with the plots and prose of Jane Austen.

ART: MARIA J. MENDOZA

MANOR CLASSICS

The Arc Manor 2008 cover opts for an Art Nouveau image that seems to present what may be Lydia Bennet as a star of the stage, ready to take London by storm. The painting's heavily worked gilded background is a far cry from the Regency's naturalism, and the voluminous drapery of the dress herald the styles of a century later. The back cover, by contrast, displays a simple design, with the famous portrait of Jane Austen set within an oval vignette.

The differences in clothing styles are readily apparent when comparing this portrait with that on the front cover.

CASSIA PRESS

Sensual and seductive, this cover image bears no relation to the story of "Jane Austen's Emma." Perhaps it intends to depict the scene wherein Mr. Perry, the apothecary, checks Harriet Smith's glands when she is home sick with a cold? No, it's simply another attempt to evoke the romance angle through a cinematographic contemporary photo, here in sepia tones that recall a nonspecific yesteryear.

Her own conduct, as well as her own heart, was before her in the same few minutes. She saw it all with a clearness that had never blessed her before.

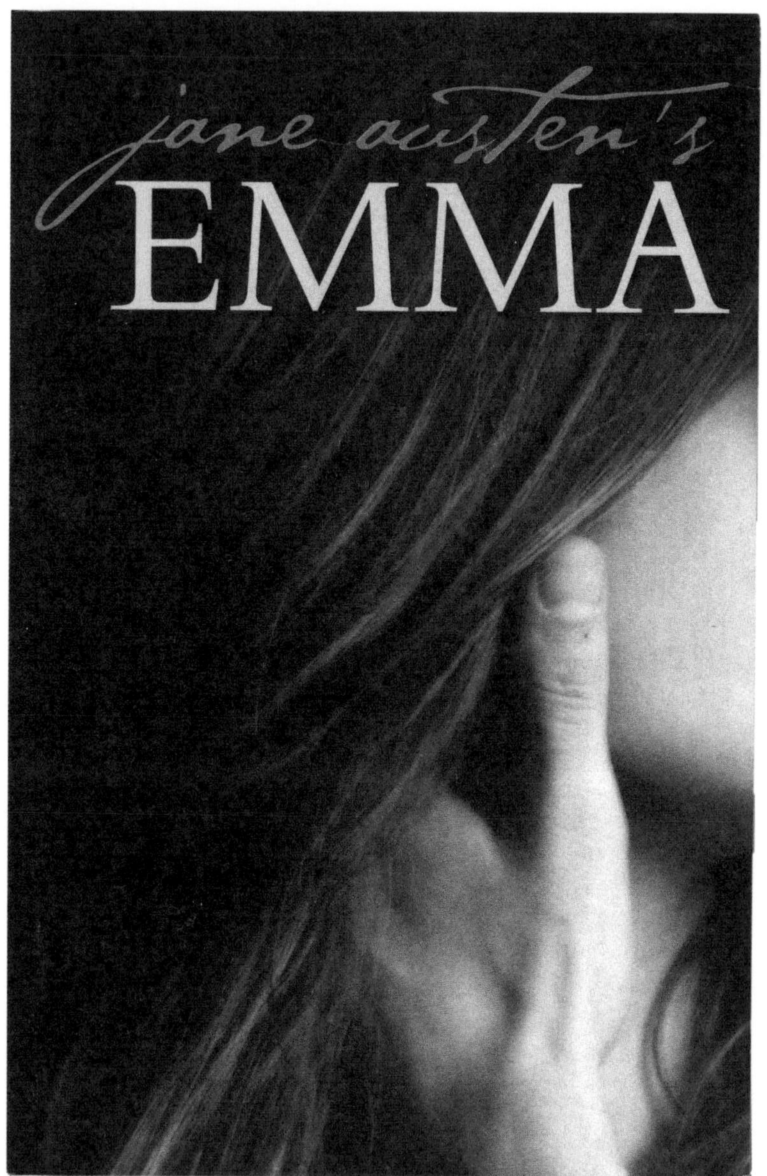

ART: GETTY IMAGES

TRANSATLANTIC PRESS

The cover of this 2012 book uses a wildly inappropriate photograph of a woman in a black hoopskirted gown, her hair loosely tied up; she looks more like a girl going to a Goth prom than a character in a Jane Austen novel. Frankly, it would work better as an action flick. To wit:

[Movie Voiceover Guy]

In a world where a woman has no power, Emma Woodhouse holds an entire neighborhood in thrall. If you get engaged to someone of whom she does not approve, she breaks it up. If you fall in love, she will interfere. If you dare to propose to her, prepare to have your heart broken.

[A woman dressed in black picks up her skirt and runs through a garden as her hair tumbles from its confines]

A whole new look at Jane Austen's most unexpected tale. This summer, don't get on the bad side of...*EMMA.*

SOHO PRESS EDITIONS

Two editions, two unique takes on the classics. *Northanger Abbey* features a gorgeous red gown and an awkward body position. (Is she sitting or squatting? We do learn in Chapter 1 that Catherine Morland played "base ball," so perhaps her position was catcher.) *Persuasion* is styled similarly (and surely not by coincidence) to the HarperTeen *Twilight*-inspired covers (page 120). This vampy edition of *Persuasion* leads one to imagine a whole different ending for Austen's last complete novel . . .

The stylized signature recalls Austen's own, here done all lowercase, e. e. cummings–style.

ART: DREAMSTIME

It was not very wonderful that Catherine, who had by nature nothing heroic about her, should prefer cricket, base ball, riding on horseback, and running about the country at the age of fourteen, to books—or at least books of information.

—Northanger Abbey

EBOOKSONTHENET

This e-book has been around for some time, though one wonders who might be tricked into purchasing it (other than, say, someone writing a book about covers of Jane Austen novels). The cover is not entirely objectionable—a random image of a woman, interesting but not especially illustrative of the story—but what is noteworthy is that both the title *and* the author's name are misspelled. As any Janeite will tell you, spelling the author's surname with an I instead of an E is a grave sin, indeed (she's not a city in Texas!). And if they can't get the title right, it is difficult to be confident that any care has been taken with the content, either.

"The merest awkward country girl, without style, or elegance, and almost without beauty.— I remember her perfectly."

DIGIVIEW ENTERTAINMENT AUDIO BOOK SERIES

Some Janeites are taking their Austen in a different format, one in which the written word becomes the spoken word. Dozens of audio versions of the novels are available, from books on tape (remember those?) to free digital downloadables narrated by crowdsourced volunteers. The cover of this 2006 recording, which comes as a set of six CDs, features laundry-detergent-esque photography. It makes one wonder if the retold story presents a revisionist take on Austen's story, in which Marianne Dashwood, driven mad by Willoughby's desertion, wanders the fields around Barton in her underclothes.

MIDDLETON CLASSICS

The combination of two late-eighteenth-century Thomas Gainsborough paintings may be a little too early for Austen's novels, which were written mostly in the early nineteenth, but the juxtaposition creates a dreamy, evocative mood. The design is in keeping with the trend among some publishers to invite readers to escape to the past, even one in which disembodied male heads gaze longingly from within a moody cloudscape.

Elizabeth, having rather expected to affront him, was amazed at his gallantry; but there was a mixture of sweetness and archness in her manner which made it difficult for her to affront anybody; and Darcy had never been so bewitched by any woman as he was by her.

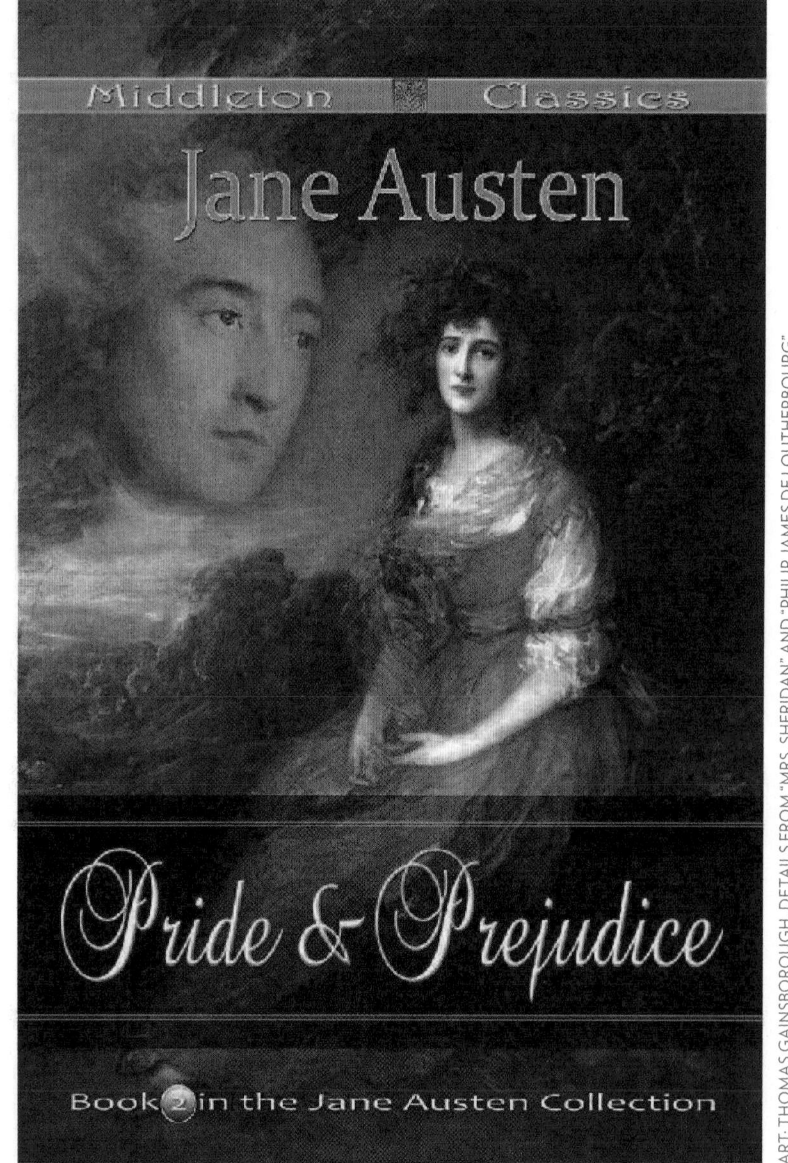

ART: THOMAS GAINSBOROUGH, DETAILS FROM "MRS. SHERIDAN" AND "PHILIP JAMES DE LOUTHERBOURG"

Modern Heirlooms

Although critiquing the less-than-great covers is a worthy pursuit in scholarship and in fun, there's a lot to praise, too: modern book designers are doing better work than ever, and some of the most recent designs are true artworks. The editions on these next pages break away from both the commercial look of the bargain paperback editions and the serious-business, oil-portrait classic hardcovers in order to breathe new life into the scenes and characters through their fresh and lively interpretations.

"Will you do me the honor of reading that letter?"

—Pride and Prejudice

ART: JILLIAN DITNER; DESIGN: EMILY MAHON

MODERN LIBRARY

In 2000, Random House's Modern Library redesigned its large-format paperback of *Pride and Prejudice*, which formerly featured an illustration by Hugh Thomson, and gave it a charming illustration by Jillian Ditner. The off-center title and bold wallpaper give this cover its modern twist even as it winks at convention with the cameo portrait on the wall. By framing the figure at the desk from behind (one assumes it's Lizzy, but then, it could be anyone), the reader is free to impose her own vision of the character.

[Jane Austen] wrote upon small sheets of paper which could easily be put away, or covered with a piece of blotting paper. There was, between the front door and the offices, a swing door which creaked when it was opened; but she objected to having this little inconvenience remedied, because it gave her notice when anyone was coming.

—J. E. AUSTEN-LEIGH, *A Memoir of Jane Austen*

DAILY TELEGRAPH EDITIONS

The U.K.'s Everyman Orion published this limited-edition set of Austen's novels in 2007 to celebrate ITV's "Austen Season." London's *Daily Telegraph* published daily coupons that could be clipped and redeemed at a certain chain of coffee shops for a free copy of the book. Each had original cover art commissioned from a different artist, and all are splendid. The folk-art feel of Richard Wilkinson's illustration for *Sense and Sensibility* evokes the close relationship of the Dashwood sisters and hints a bit at the plot besides, whereas Bernie Reid's cover for *Pride and Prejudice* takes an edgy approach to the iconic pose of courtship with graffiti-inspired stencils. Brett Ryder's illustration combines a Victorian, Edward Gorey–esque cast of black-clad characters, a butterfly with groovy sixties brightness, and snaking roses that invoke Monty Python's absurd cut-and-paste animation style. It's an old-is-new pastiche, but for *Mansfield Park*, it works. David Downton's elegant and understated charcoal-colored watercolor (page 138) captures Emma Woodhouse's elegance as she leans negligently on a chair (and no doubt plots her next program for improving her friends' lives). Alan Baker's unfinished but dynamic tableau visually echoes the lost-and-found-again love story of Anne Elliot and Captain Wentworth in *Persuasion*, while Jeff Fisher's handwritten cover sets the final sentence of *Northanger Abbey* atop a swooning lady. The result is a bit of metafictional cheekery: the book about books is now using its own words to invite judgment on itself.

ART: RICHARD WILKINSON

ART: BERNIE REID

ART: BRETT RYDER

ART: DAVID DOWNTON

ART: ALAN BAKER

I leave it to be settled by whomsoever it may concern, whether the tendency of this work be altogether to recommend parental tyranny or reward filial disobedience.

NORTHANGER ABBEY
Jane Austen

ART: JEFF FISHER

ART: CORALIE BICKFORD-SMITH

PENGUIN HARDCOVER CLASSICS

Penguin made its reputation on paperback editions but added the Hardcover Classics to its lineup a few years ago. The result is truly a book as covetable object. As with this 2009 copy of *Sense and Sensibility*, the covers are made of sturdy linen and stamped with an attractive motif. The books include scholarly introductions and other supplemental material. These are "keeper" editions for the general reader, and they make gorgeous collectibles.

The allover plant pattern recalls the early-20th-century Art Nouveau textile designs.

WORDCLOUD CLASSICS

This Canterbury Classics edition from 2013 sports a faux leather cover with an embossed word cloud, such as one might find on a blog or website, that arranges phrases from the book in an every-direction cluster. An all-typography cover is unusual for Austen, but the journal-like feel of this volume and the personal, emotional tenor of the quotes avoid skewing too sterile, making this conceit a fitting, if surprising, choice.

If I was wrong in yielding to persuasion once, remember that it was to persuasion exerted on the side of safety, not of risk. When I yielded, I thought it was to duty; but no duty could be called in aid here. In marrying a man indifferent to me, all risk would have been incurred and all duty violated.

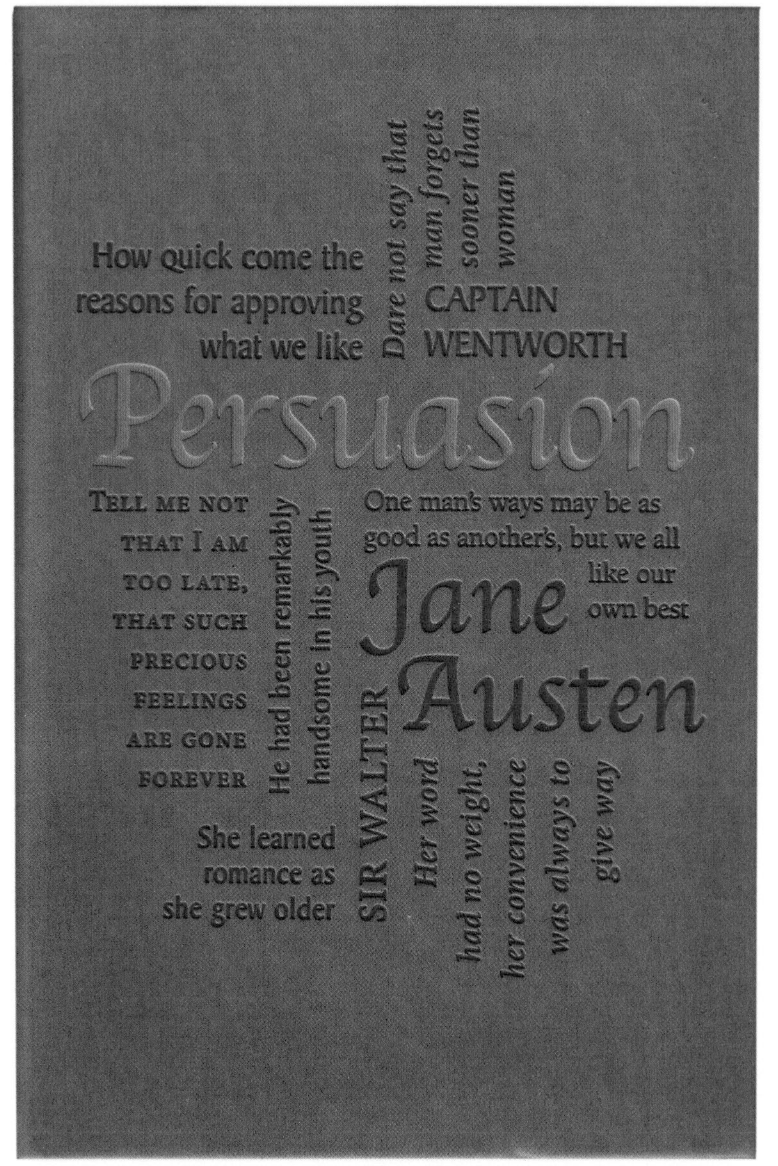

He drew out a letter from under the scattered paper, placed it before Anne with eyes of glowing entreaty fixed on her for a time, and hastily collecting his gloves, was again out of the room.

—*Persuasion*

CLASSIC LINES

The cover of this edition of *Emma*, published in 2012 by Splinter/ Sterling Publishing, fairly swooshes by with an impressionistic single-color wash painting by the fashion illustrator Sara Singh. Fluid lines and handwritten lettering invite an enjoyable, leisurely reading. There are no scholarly extras, but this large-format paperback is one that any fashionista would be proud to own.

ART: SARA SINGH; DESIGN: AURA LEWIS

ART: JILLIAN TAMAKI; DESIGN: PAUL BUCKLEY

PENGUIN THREADS

Another deluxe edition from Penguin, this one from 2011 (this page and overleaf) is absolutely, meticulously beautiful. The carefully stitched multicolor design of a bonneted girl is stunning—and when you open the cover, the back of the needlework shows on the back of the board! The fiber artist Jillian Tamaki drew the designs and then handstitched each one; the covers are sculpt-embossed to retain the texture of the embroidery. But this is more than just an unrelated gimmick: Jane Austen was an avid needleworker, specializing in the same kind of satin stitch as is used here. Her relatives often spoke of the neatness of her work. Examples of her needlework survive and are on display at the Jane Austen's House Museum in Chawton, Hampshire.

"ONE HALF OF
THE WORLD CANNOT
UNDERSTAND THE
PLEASURES OF
THE OTHER."
A Penguin Book
Literature
U.S. $16.00
CAN. $18.50
ISBN 978-0-14-310646-3
51600
9 780143 106463
EAN

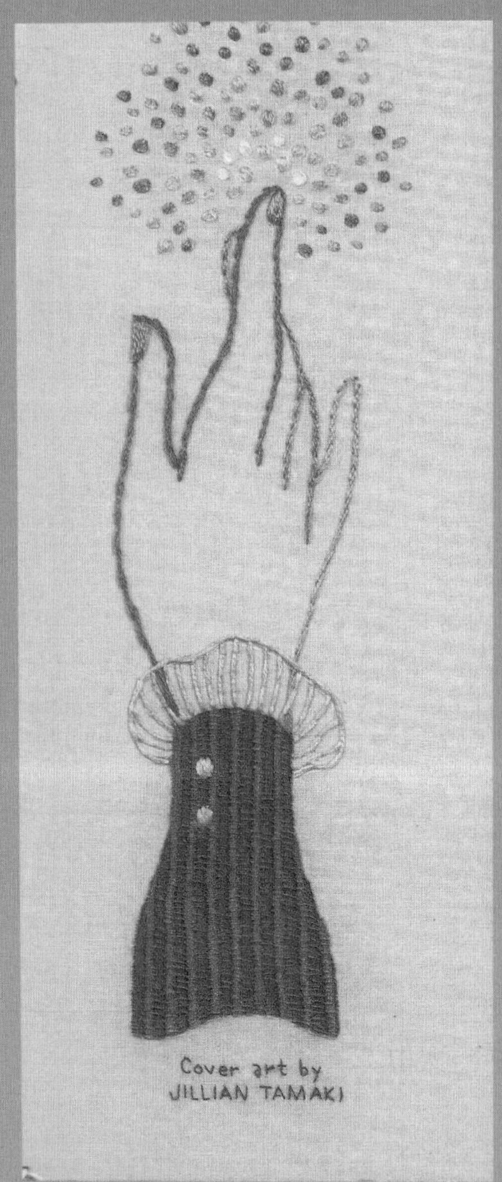
Cover art by
JILLIAN TAMAKI

PENGUIN CLASSICS DELUXE EDITIONS

Continuing the trend of upmarket illustrated covers are these editions from Penguin Classics Deluxe from 2009–11. Fashion illustrator Ruben Toledo drew the cover for *Pride and Prejudice*, and author Audrey Niffenegger (of *The Time Traveler's Wife* fame) drew the covers for *Sense and Sensibility* and *Persuasion*. Rather than attempt to faithfully represent scenes from the book, as did many of the early 1990s paperback editions, these larger-format softcovers take a more interpretive route, using symbolic tableaus for a show-don't-tell effect that leaves something to the imagination (and creates the kind of intangible value meriting a higher price point). The handwritten titles add to the well-desgined caché—not quite heirloom editions, but not beach reading, either.

ART: RUBEN TOLEDO; DESIGN: SABRINA BOWERS

ART: AUDREY NIFFENEGGER

ART: AUDREY NIFFENEGGER

MARVEL COMICS

Several of Austen's texts have been published as graphic novels for Marvel, with the original adapted by the romance novelist Nancy Butler and several artists. The covers are lovely: Sonny Liew's *Sense and Sensibility* (2010) captures the lively and cheerful (though complicated) trials of the Dashwoods, and Julian Totino Tedesco's exquisite portrait makes for an eerily Gothic *Northanger Abbey* (2012). Miss Morland would approve!

ART: SONNY LIEW

ART: JULIAN TOTINO TEDESCO

"WHEN A YOUNG LADY IS TO BE A HEROINE...SOMETHING MUST AND WILL HAPPEN TO THROW A HERO IN HER WAY."

Lovingly adapted from Jane Austen's most humorous work, Marvel Comics is proud to present literature lover Catherine Morland's quest to be the leading lady of her own great romance. Can real life prove the equal of the Gothic novels she finds so enchanting? Can Catherine find true love amid the fictions of others and her own wild imagination? And what dread secrets lie in wait in Northanger Abbey itself?

Award-winning author Nancy Butler continues her quest to reinvent Jane Austen's Regency world in the Mighty Marvel Manner. With exquisite illustrations from Janet Lee, 19th-century England comes alive like never before. Discover — along with Catherine Morland — that while truth may not be stranger than fiction, it can be no less surprising!

Collecting *Northanger Abbey* #1-5.

ISBN 978-0-7851-6440-1
$14.99 US $16.99 CAN

MARVEL

MARVEL.COM

ART: LARS LEETARU; DESIGN: DOOGIE HORNER

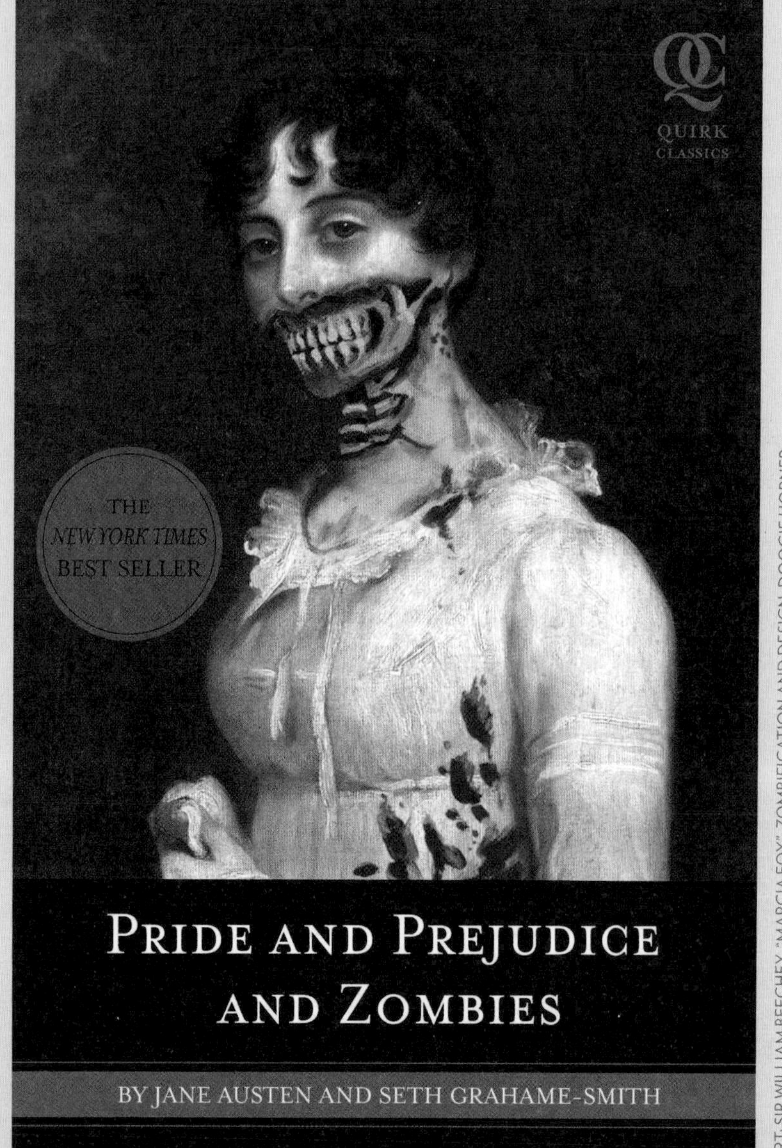

ART: SIR WILLIAM BEECHEY, "MARCIA FOX"; ZOMBIFICATION AND DESIGN: DOOGIE HORNER

ART: SIR WILLIAM BEECHEY, "MARCIA FOX"; ZOMBIFICATION AND DESIGN: DOOGIE HORNER

QUIRK CLASSICS

Billed as "The Classic Regency Romance—Now with Ultraviolent Zombie Mayhem!" these remixed editions roared, lumbered, and slithered onto the scene in 2009. Austen's original text was altered and expanded to include all the gory details readers didn't know they'd been missing. The series was a hit, reaching #1 on the *New York Times* Best-Seller List and spawning sequels, knock-offs, and plans for a movie. In keeping with the old-meets-gruesome theme, the illustration for the "PPZ" cover reimagines the portrait of Marcia Fox by Sir William Beechey (page 66) with blood-encrusted mandibles and glowing eyes. Other volumes in the series featured original paintings by Lars Leetaru.

It is a truth universally acknowledged that a zombie in possession of brains must be in want of more brains.

—PRIDE AND PREJUDICE AND ZOMBIES

PULP! THE CLASSICS

The hilarious cover on this faux-pulp edition of *Pride and Prejudice*, published in 2013 by Oldcastle Books, fooled a few people into thinking it was a genuine 1950s edition. But the truly alert Janeite would recognize the likeless of Colin Firth as Mr. Darcy, deducing that the image could not predate the mid-1990s. Playing with conventions of sensationalistic hardboiled novels, the bold lettering, rugged (and shirtless!) hero with dangling cigarette, and contrived surface wear create one of the better remixes. Lock up your daughters!

ART: DAVID MANN

Austen for the Littlest Readers

"You done nobly," he says. "You're bringin' forth abundant fruit, like a good Janeite."

—"THE JANEITES" by Rudyard Kipling

It is a truth universally acknowledged that we Janeites tend to proselytize. We can discuss our favorites loudly and at length and purchase extra copies of Austen's novels just to have them on hand to pass to interested parties, especially young people discovering her work for the first time. And though many of us are scrupulous and pass on only the whole, intact, uncondensed texts to the next generation of Austen fans, that hasn't forestalled the publication of abridged editions for younger readers—and now even board books.

BABYLIT

The Little Miss Austen series from Gibbs Smith presents adorably illustrated board-book primers that make wonderful gifts for new Janeite parents. The kid-friendly colors and chunky package are perfect for little ones, and they've got an educational bent as well: *Pride and Prejudice* is a counting book, and *Sense and Sensibility* is an opposites primer, both fitting themes.

ART AND DESIGN: ALISON OLIVER

ART: JACK AND HOLMAN WANG; DESIGN: SARA GILLINGHAM STUDIO

COZY CLASSICS

"Give a kid a classic!" Published by Simply Read Books, this series of board books features photographs of felt figures illustrating scenes in the novel, each scene accompanied by a single word such as "sisters," "sick," or "mean." The cross-stitch and needlework theme is appropriate to the stories, it's true. Note the faithful (and darling!) line of mud on the hem of Lizzy's dress on this 2012 edition of *Pride and Prejudice*.

"I hope you saw her petticoat, six inches deep in mud, I am absolutely certain; and the gown which had been let down to hide it not doing its office."

GREAT ILLUSTRATED CLASSICS

Baronet Books' 1997 version of *Pride and Prejudice* is a sturdy hardback with black-and-white line drawings throughout. Though longer than most other adaptations, the text has been extensively rewritten in much simpler language that's disappointingly reductive in the eyes of most Austen loyalists. The cover image of, apparently, Elizabeth and Jane Bennet is painted in the same bright, photo-realistic style as appears on popular tween books of the era, likely with an eye toward attracting fans of *Sweet Valley High* and *Baby-Sitters Club* (the copy on the back similarly emphasizes the relatable theme of sisterly friendship rather than the "grown-up" idea of marriage). And though no gentlemen are in view here, drawings on the inside depict male figures of appropriately chiseled jaws (Mr. Wickham, in particular, is tall and gorgeous in his uniform; no doubt this edition would be Lydia's favorite).

ART: JOSEPH MIRALLES

ART: ANN KRONHEIMER

REAL READS

This series, published by Skyview Books, an imprint of Windmill Books, rewrites Austen's novels for a middle-grade audience. *Sense and Sensibility* (2009) is written in the first person from youngest sister Margaret Dashwood's point of view, and it has attractive color illustrations throughout. As with the Great Illustrated Classics, the image reflects contemporary trends in cover design for the middle-school reader: vibrant eye-catching pinks on top, soft and dainty illustrations of pretty heroines beneath.

Margaret, the other sister, was a good-humored, well-disposed girl; but as she had already imbibed a good deal of Marianne's romance, without having much of her sense, she did not, at thirteen, bid fair to equal her sisters at a more advanced period of life.

RAINTREE PUBLISHERS

This rewritten abridgement from 1981 is beautifully illustrated with full-color drawings by Helen Cogancherry, and unlike other books of its type, it is a hardback. One can imagine this edition being a gift for a young Janeite-in-training.

"My dear Eliza, he must be in love with you, or he would never have called on us in this familiar way."

ART: HELEN COGANCHERRY

OXFORD BOOKWORMS LIBRARY

Pride and Prejudice, rewritten and abridged for two different generations. The cover of the older version (*below*), dated 1995, shows the faces of Jennifer Ehle and Colin Firth in what appears to be a Lizzy-Darcy Venn diagram. The newer version (*left*), from 2007, shows Keira Knightley as Elizabeth departing from Pemberley. The easier-reading text and back cover blurbs of both books are identical; clearly the publishers knew that a cover that fits its young audience's current image of the book's characters is key to selling its edition.

ART: BBC PICTURE ARCHIVES

SADDLEBACK CLASSICS AND TIMELESS CLASSICS

Oh, how charming! Mr. and Mrs. Darcy went to the Grand Canyon on their honeymoon! Or so one would think from this 2011 abridgement of *Pride and Prejudice* (*below*). Both of these editions come from Saddleback Educational Publishing, which renamed its line of rewritten classics and updated the cover with an anachronistic illustration that seems more at home in the American West than in Regency England. At least on the earlier abridged version of 2003 (*right*) the artist got the period correct.

The sepia tones and Wild West imagery are a puzzling choice for an Austen novel.

ART: BLACK EAGLE PRODUCTIONS

The Complete Austen

He immediately offered to fetch her others; all that his library afforded.
"And I wish my collection were larger for your benefit and my own credit; but I am an idle fellow, and though I have not many, I have more than I ever look into."

—MR. BINGLEY in *Pride and Prejudice*

Jane Austen wrote only six novels, so it's easy for publishers to collect them into a single volume, even throwing in a few extras, including text from her other works. These are big books with small print. The more handsome editions make lovely gifts for someone new to Austen's oeuvre. And, in a pinch, they make splendid doorstops.

MODERN LIBRARY

This 1978 library copy from Random House has a delightfully of-the-era design. The bold statement typography doesn't pull any punches: rather than conjure up images of roses or swooning couples, it is stark and simple, with a kind of does-what-it-says-on-the-tin directness. The swash font was a popular choice at the time, with the most famous Bookman face designed by typographer Edward Benguiat in the mid-seventies.

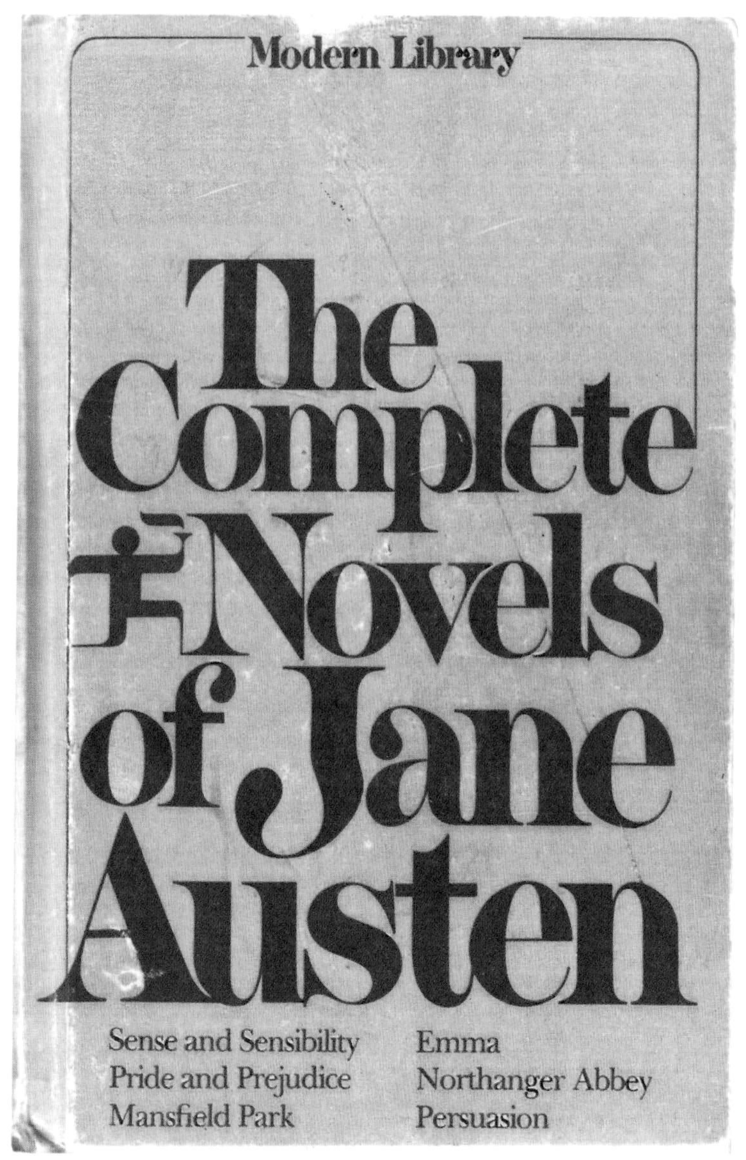

BARNES AND NOBLE

This beautiful, faux-leather-bound edition is meant for collectors, with its embossed foil cover, intricate floral design, ribbon bookmark, and gold-edged pages. As with many Austen compendiums, the small type is set on thin paper to minimize bulkiness. The collection inside includes *Lady Susan*, hence the seven novels of the title.

GREAT ENGLISH CLASSICS

Penguin always seems to offer one of these all-in-one volumes, though the design has grown more sophisticated over the years. The U.K. edition from 1983 (*right*) is a thing of its time, with square sans-serif type, the famous silhouette of Jane Austen, and a spray of flowers, almost as an afterthought—rather plain and workmanlike, on the whole. The U.S. edition (*below*) from the same year is softer, centered with a medallion featuring the painting of Jane Austen by James Andrews that was commissioned for the 1869 *Memoir* (and which recently sold at auction for £164,500, or $270,000).

The American version got a bonus, *Lady Susan*, bringing the total of "English Classics" to seven.

ART: JAMES ANDREWS, "PORTRAIT OF JANE AUSTEN"

ART: LESLIE HOWELL

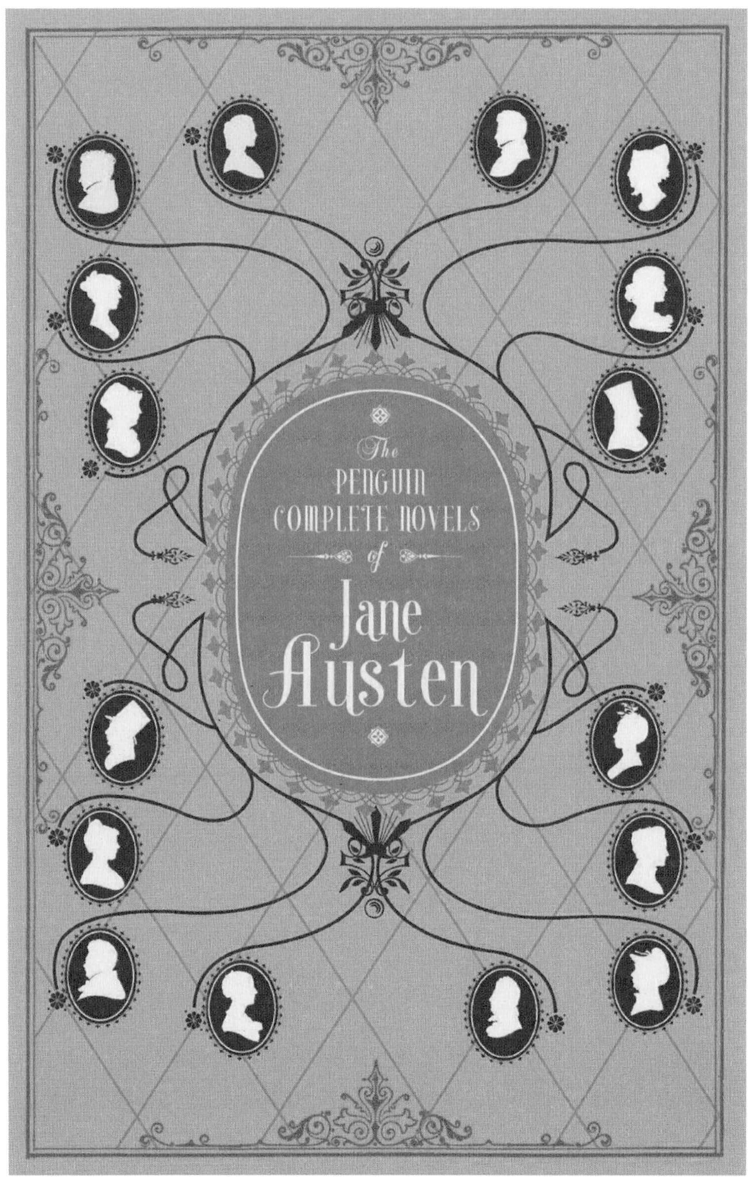

PENGUIN COMPLETE NOVELS

The latest edition, published in 2013, is the most elegant yet, with a soft pink background and cameo illustrations that resemble a family tree. The "branches" reflect both the tangled relationships in Austen's stories and the way the characters are joined together in a single, large volume.

PENGUIN CLASSICS DELUXE EDITION

This 2006 edition includes the novella *Lady Susan* as well as the six main novels, along with an introduction by Karen Joy Fowler, author of the novel *The Jane Austen Book Club*. The tiered pattern approach is not only attractive but also clever: one band per novel, plus one for the title and a small image detail to hint at romance. The nineteenth-century painting peeking out—*The Kiss* by G. Baldry—is a popular one; it has graced the front of John Polidori's novel *The Vampyre* and a number of modern Austen "sequels." It also served as inspiration to illustrate the mash-up novel *Android Karenina*.

ART: G. BALDRY, DETAIL FROM "THE KISS"; WALLPAPERS: HAMILTON WESTON WALLPAPERS LTD.; DESIGN: KELLY BLAIR

"Oh! I am delighted with the book! I should like to spend my whole life reading it."

—Northanger Abbey

KNICKERBOCKER CLASSICS

This lovely slipcased edition, published in 2013 by Race Point, is a splendid addition to any Janeite's library. The design is plain but elegant, with the author's signature embossed in gold on the slipcase (*below*)—a considerably more upmarket approach than many bargain-rate complete collections. A brief scholarly introduction is also included.

BY "A LADY"

Few of her readers knew even her name, and none knew more of her than her name. I doubt whether it would be possible to mention any other author of note, whose personal obscurity was so complete.

—J. E. AUSTEN-LEIGH, nephew of Jane Austen, in *A Memoir of Jane Austen*

At the time of Jane Austen's birth in 1775, writing for money was still a new idea. The upper classes scorned paid employment, and authorship was no exception. Though writers such as Samuel Richardson and Henry Fielding made it acceptable for men to earn a living publishing fiction, for women the practice was dismissed as less than genteel. Moreover, the fame—or, rather, the notoriety—enjoyed by popular authors was something that a woman of Austen's class would wish to avoid. Nonetheless, women authored most of the novels published in Austen's time, but because of the social pressures, most published anonymously. Either that or they felt compelled to write servile and self-effacing forewords in which they apologized for putting themselves forward and explained the financial reversals that had driven them to such straits.

Austen resolutely kept her name off her books during her lifetime: *Sense and Sensibility* featured only the credit "By a Lady" on its title page, and her later books carried the byline "By the author of" her previous titles. She disliked celebrity and tried to keep her authorship a secret even after it had been discovered. After her death in 1817, her relatives worked hard to maintain her image as a gifted amateur (much to the consternation of modern scholars who think that such a suggestion is untrue and belittles Austen's achievements).

However, as early as 1814, amid the surging popularity of *Pride and Prejudice*, Austen's authorship was an open secret. Her brother Henry was partly to blame; as a banker, he met many prominent people and was happy to tell anyone who praised the novels that they were written by his sister. By the time *Emma* was published in 1815, even the Prince Regent, who was a fan, knew the author's identity. In fact, when he heard Jane was in London, he sent his librarian to "invite" her to dedicate her next book to His Highness (surely the kind of invitation that cannot be refused!).

Other female authors, such as Frances Burney and Ann Radcliffe, had given up publishing anonymously when it became clear their fame had reached a height that their very identities were selling points: their names on the covers translated into higher sales. Had Austen lived longer, she perhaps would have given up her anonymity—especially if "Jane Austen" had become in her lifetime the brand that it is today.

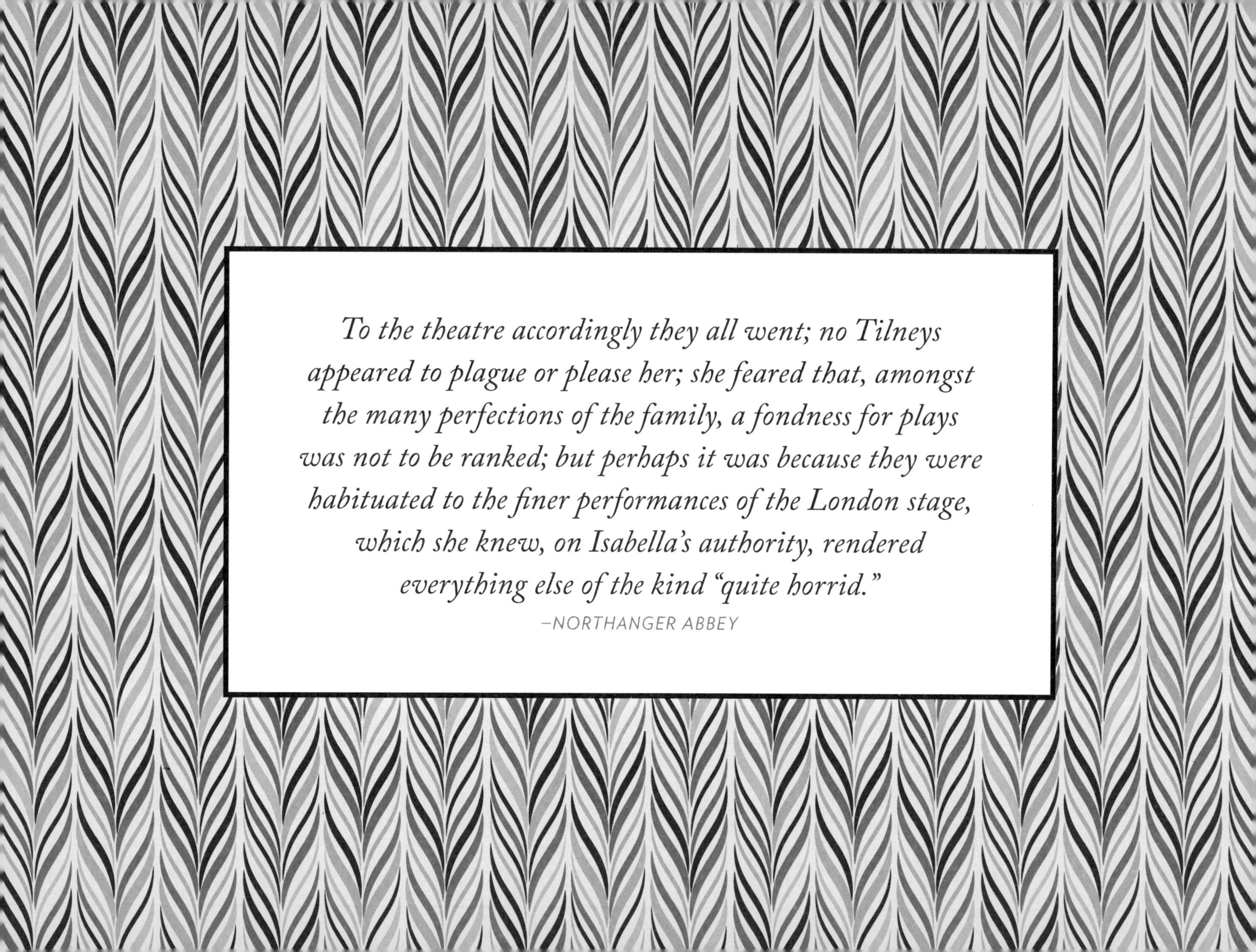
To the theatre accordingly they all went; no Tilneys appeared to plague or please her; she feared that, amongst the many perfections of the family, a fondness for plays was not to be ranked; but perhaps it was because they were habituated to the finer performances of the London stage, which she knew, on Isabella's authority, rendered everything else of the kind "quite horrid."
—NORTHANGER ABBEY

CHAPTER FIVE

Stars of the Silver Screen

You found him in the dark. Projected onto a movie screen or emanating from the television in your living room, there he was: your favorite Jane Austen hero made flesh. Perhaps it was a first meeting, which then led you to his counterpart on the printed page. Or perhaps you simply wanted a memento of that charged moment.

Unsurprisingly, film and television adaptations of Austen's novels have been around almost as long as film and television (though some were less than thorough; a television movie of *Pride and Prejudice* from 1938, though hailed as "charming," lasted a breezy 55 minutes.) The first big Hollywood production of an Austen novel came in 1940, starring Greer Garson and Laurence Olivier. By the 1990s, a string of wildly successful big- and small-screen adaptations, full of lush period detail (no Southern belle ballgowns), were in the works. Nearly all had an equally lush movie tie-in edition to go with them.

The onscreen adaptations of Austen's novels often tell us more about the time in which they were filmed than about Regency England. Everything from haircuts to hemlines can be tweaked or fudged to appeal to the tastes of a contemporary moviegoing public. Greer Garson's impeccably coiffed silver-screen version of Elizabeth Bennet, for example, is a world away from Keira Knightley's windswept, six-inches-very-much-in-mud take on the character.

Yet each iteration proves anew what all Janeites already know: these stories truly are for all time.

MGM

GROSSET AND DUNLAP

As the cover proclaims: "The age-old story thrillingly brought to the screen by MGM." On the heels of a little film from the previous year—*Gone with the Wind*—producers bumped the setting of Austen's story to the 1850s to capitalize on moviegoers' enthusiasm for puffed sleeves and romantic melodrama. Filmed in glorious black and white and complete with ludicrously anachronistic costumes, this movie seems quaint to modern eyes. But at the time it was a pretty big deal for Austen fans to see one of her novels on the big screen.

The back cover of this movie tie-in book features the stars who "masterfully portray the characters . . . made from this moving novel of a romantic period."

BBC

FONTANA

After MGM's 1940 take on *Pride and Prejudice*, Hollywood would then ignore Jane Austen for another fifty years. Back in England, however, the BBC produced telefilms based on her novels with steady regularity throughout the twentieth century. "Auntie Beeb" adapted each of the novels in the 1970s and 1980s, and these are now the earliest television adaptations available on DVD. Shoestring production values notwithstanding, the 1980 BBC miniseries of *Pride and Prejudice* is considered by Janeites to be one of the most faithful adaptations. American fans watched the miniseries just as avidly on PBS, and many probably picked up this companion paperback as well.

A&E/BBC

PENGUIN MODERN LIBRARY

Around the same time as Columbia Pictures was releasing *Sense and Sensibility*, the U.S. channel A&E and the BBC collaborated on what is perhaps the most famous and beloved Austen film adaptation of all time: the 1995 *Pride and Prejudice* miniseries starring Jennifer Ehle as Elizabeth Bennet and Colin Firth as Mr. Darcy. Befitting the popularity of this series, an embarrassment of tie-in riches is available. Penguin published a trade paperback of the novel in the United Kingdom (*right*), and in the United States, Modern Library put a new, Firth-centric dustjacket on its existing hardback edition (*below*).

ART: STUART WOOD

A&E/BBC

MODERN LIBRARY

A couple years later, the same group that produced the *Pride and Prejudice* miniseries adapted *Emma* for television, with Kate Beckinsale in the lead role. Another new dust jacket was commissioned for the Modern Library edition, again showing scenes of the stars in superposition.

ART: COURTESY MERIDIAN BROADCASTING LTD.; DESIGN: SJI ASSOCIATES

MIRAMAX
HYPERION

Nearly concurrent with the production of the television version of *Emma*, in 1996 Miramax produced a feature film adaptation of the novel starring Gwyneth Paltrow. The company's publishing arm, Hyperion, duly put out a trade paperback tie-in edition featuring an immediately recognizable image from one of the movie posters.

Emma Woodhouse, handsome, clever, and rich, with a comfortable home and happy disposition, seemed to unite some of the best blessings of existence; and had lived nearly twenty-one years in the world with very little to distress or vex her.

ART: MICHAEL O'NEIL

ART: DAN BROWN

ENRICHED CLASSICS

As we collected books and scoured used bookstores and Internet databases for more and different editions of Austen's novel, we were amused by a phenomenon we had not known existed—covers clearly designed to appeal to fans of the films without actually using images from the film. For instance, Pocket Books' 2005 *Emma* cover clearly invokes Gwyneth Paltrow, even if she is not holding her teacup.

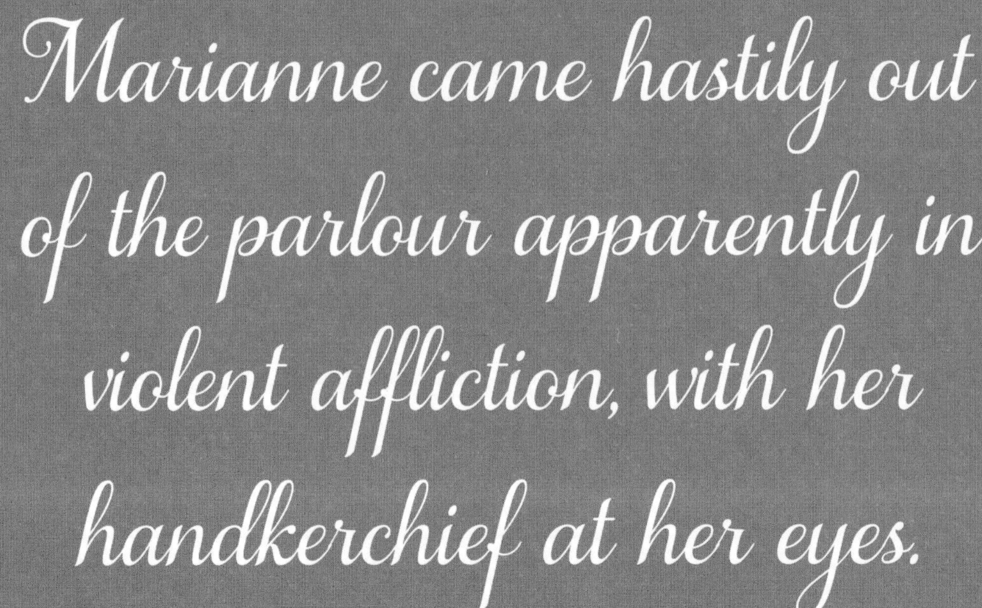

—*Sense and Sensibility*

ART: CLIVE COOTE

COLUMBIA PICTURES

SIGNET

The tie-in for the 1995 adaptation of *Sense and Sensibility*, starring Emma Thompson and Kate Winslet, reproduces the movie poster on the cover and includes black-and-white stills from the film inside. Thompson, who was tapped to write the screenplay based on her work in sketch comedy (and only later picked to star as Elinor Dashwood) won an Academy Award for the adaptation.

BLOOMSBURY METHUEN

Although the 1995 adaptation of *Persuasion* is thoroughly wonderful, there is sadly no tie-in edition of the novel. Disappointed fans must content ourselves with a published edition of the script, whose cover features a striking full-bleed photo of Amanda Root as Anne Elliot.

Whether former feelings were to be renewed must be brought to the proof; former times must undoubtedly be brought to the recollection of each; they could not but be reverted to.

ART: BBC

ART: MIRAMAX FILMS

MIRAMAX

HYPERION

In 1999, Miramax released a controversial big-screen adaptation of *Mansfield Park*. Writers added new material, both to liven up the main character and to reflect modern postcolonial literary criticism about the role of slavery and feminism in the novel. The film tanked at the box office, and most Janeites were either bewildered or contemptuous. Unfortunately, rather than admitting that it might just have been a bad film, studio honchos saw its failure as a sign that This Austen Thing Has Passed. In any event, Hyperion released a tie-in edition featuring a salacious close-up kiss between two anonymous people and a tiny thumbnail of the movie poster featuring Frances O'Connor as Fanny Price. At best, the rather tone-deaf cover reflects a cluelessness about the story; at worst, it shows a kind of contempt for the book and its readers.

UNIVERSAL STUDIOS

PENGUIN

The next six years are known informally to Janeites as the Dark Years, when no films were made, or really even contemplated, apparently because of the failure of the *Mansfield Park* adaptation. But around 2003, Internet rumblings began to stir about a new big-screen version of *Pride and Prejudice*. Excitement was at a fever pitch, and the 2005 film starring Keira Knightley and Matthew Macfadyen as Elizabeth and Mr. Darcy was a box-office hit. In contrast to the lush period style of the 1990s adaptations, this version gave Austen's tidy world a dose of "gritty realism" and a smattering of Brontëan melodrama (not to mention a popular young star in Knightley), all in an effort to reach a new generation of viewers. Though many stalwart Janeites disliked the revisionist result, the film garnered multiple Academy Award nominations: one for Knightley, and one each for art direction, costume design, and original score. Penguin dutifully released a tie-in edition featuring images from the movie poster on the cover.

ART: THOMAS SULLY, DETAIL FROM "PORTRAIT OF ELLEN AND MARY MCILVAINE"

MASTERPIECE

PENGUIN

One successful film begat many more, and ITV and the BBC in the U.K. and PBS in the U.S. planned to broadcast collections of Austen adaptations both old and new. This time, austerity—rather than exhaustive cross-promotion—seemed to be the watchword. Though PBS's Masterpiece series showed adaptations of all six Austen novels in 2008, no publisher put out new tie-in editions. They just slapped a sticker on the existing Penguin Classics editions, in case anyone was looking.

PBS/BBC

PENGUIN

Despite some criticism from Janeites, the new crop of adaptations has been successful. In 2009 the BBC and PBS collaborated on a new miniseries of *Emma* starring Romola Garai. This time they did the movie tie-in properly, with a full-bleed cover photo featuring the lead actress as Miss Woodhouse.

Now, it so happened that in spite of Emma's resolution of never marrying, there was something in the name, in the idea of Mr. Frank Churchill, which always interested her.

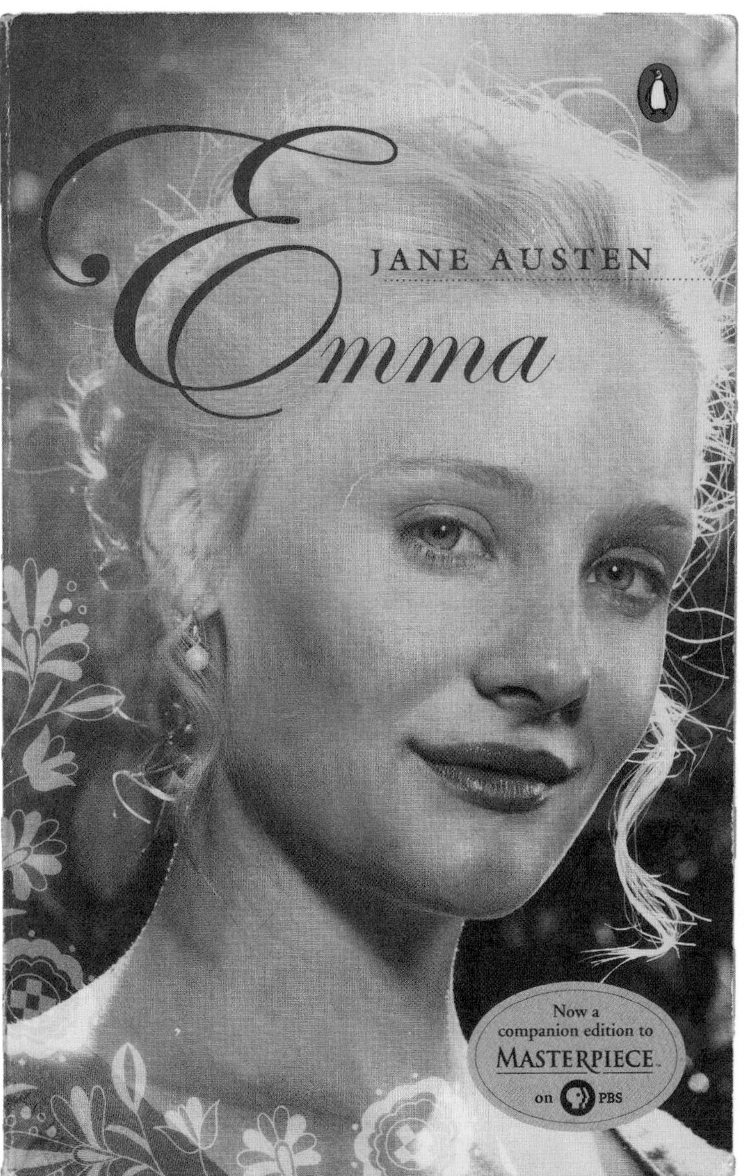

ART: DAVID TENNI/BBC FOR MASTERPIECE; DESIGN: C. CLAIRE DESIGN

FASHION PLATE

Most people familiar with Jane Austen's novels, or the films adapted from them, have an idea of the proper Regency costume for her female characters: a high-waisted, low-cut floor-length gown that hangs close to the body, made of white or light-colored cotton with short puffy sleeves. However, the composition and publication of the novels extended over twenty-plus years, and during that time fashions changed. It's easy to pick out an obvious anachronism, such as the huge hoopskirts gracing the heroines of *Pride and Prejudice* in both the 1940 film adaptation and the Signet Classics cover (pages 172 and 64). But the true enthusiast can date a particular costume to within five or ten years.

At the end of the eighteenth century, the French Revolution affected fashion both on the Continent and across the Channel. The stiff brocades and formality of the court were dispensed with (along with the aristocrats), and styles became simpler. Men's clothing was inspired by English country wear, with coats cut away in the front to facilitate horseback riding as well as the breeches and boots worn for that activity. Also introduced were pantaloons, or trousers, worn mostly for less formal occasions.

Women's clothing changed too; cuts softened and grew rounder, following the contours of the figure. Gowns had a natural waistline, sometimes highlighted with a tied sash, and skirts were still fairly full. Young women wore their hair down, in cascades of curls, or sometimes cropped close to the head. Austen wrote her first two novels, *Sense and Sensibility* and *Pride and Prejudice*, around this time, and the costumes for the 1995 and 2005 films (pages 174 and 182) accurately reflect the era, with tweaks to accommodate modern tastes.

Around 1800, an enthusiasm for neoclassical architecture spilled over into women's fashions. Simple, close-fitting gowns with high waists and short sleeves made of muslin in white or light pastels recalled ancient Greek statuary. Hair was worn in an updo with side curls. The painting used for the cover of the Oxford World's Classics edition of *Catharine and Other Writings* (page 79) is an example of this style.

Clothing became more elaborate in the early 1800s. After 1810, daywear designs featured long sleeves, ribbons and fancy trimmings, high ruffled collars, and intricate flounces; colors, too, were more varied, though white and light-colored gowns were still popular. Examples can be seen on the Dover Thrift edition of *Pride and Prejudice* (page 87); the Signet Classic *Northanger Abbey* (page 88); and the Oxford World's Classics cover of *Mansfield Park* (page 114). Evening wear can be seen on the cover of the Wordsworth Classics *Persuasion* (page 85). The elaborate flounces on the gowns were very much a thing of this later period.

Only one of Austen's novels, *Persuasion*, was given a specific setting: late summer 1814 to February 1815, coinciding with the period of peace during Napoleon's confinement on Elba. The 1995 film adaptation (page 180) gets the costumes nearly perfect.

After 1820, waistlines began to drop and skirts became fuller, as in the fashion plate on the cover of the Romance Classics *Emma* (page 92). Gentleman's clothing also shows a metamorphosis to a hat with a taller brim and an overcoat with a pronounced waistline. By the 1830s, the simple Regency gown was no more, replaced with full skirts, necklines set wide on the shoulders, and giant puffed sleeves, as seen on the cover of the Oxford World's Classics edition of *Pride and Prejudice* (page 79).

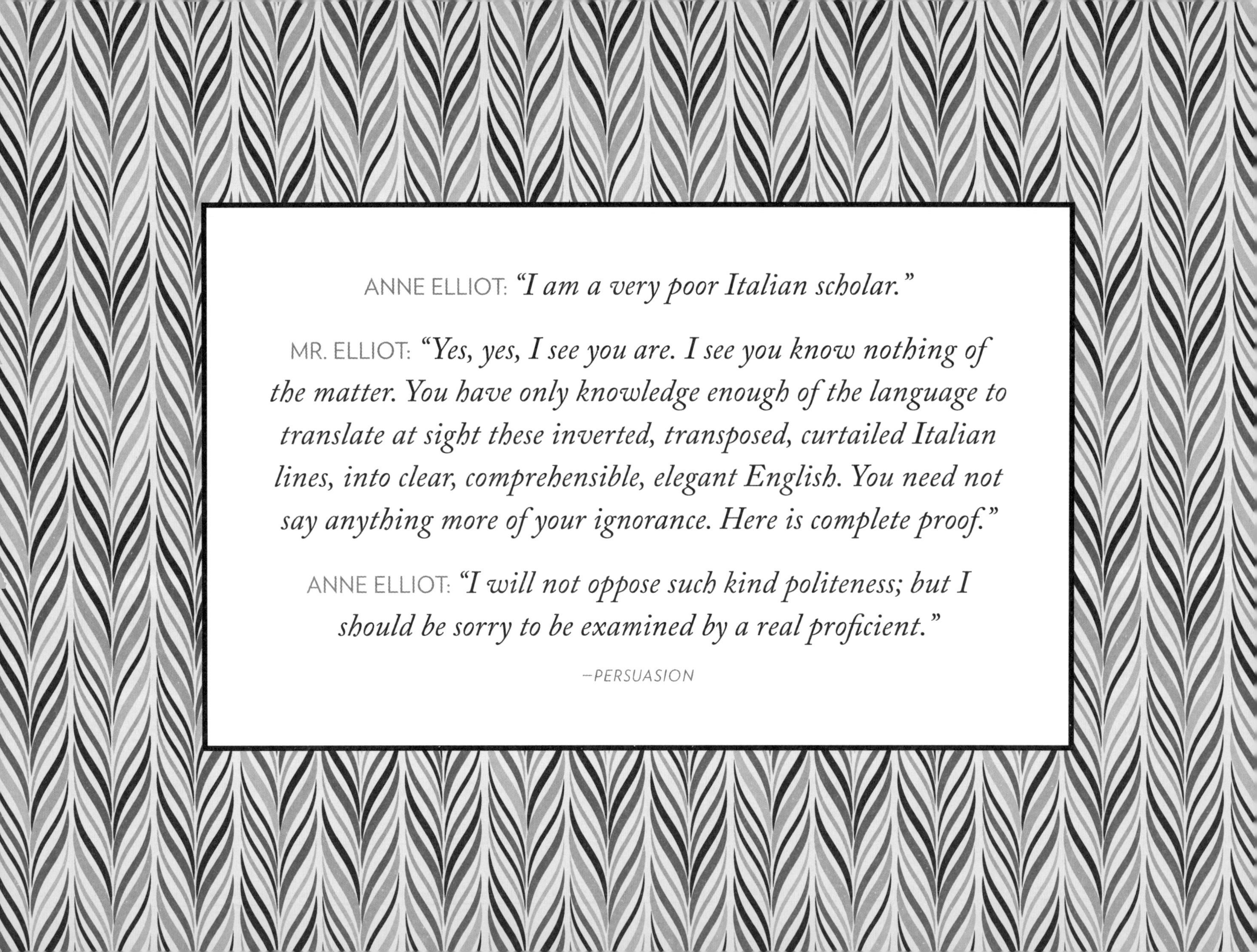

ANNE ELLIOT: *"I am a very poor Italian scholar."*

MR. ELLIOT: *"Yes, yes, I see you are. I see you know nothing of the matter. You have only knowledge enough of the language to translate at sight these inverted, transposed, curtailed Italian lines, into clear, comprehensible, elegant English. You need not say anything more of your ignorance. Here is complete proof."*

ANNE ELLIOT: *"I will not oppose such kind politeness; but I should be sorry to be examined by a real proficient."*

—*PERSUASION*

CHAPTER SIX

A Thorough Knowledge of the Modern Languages

The novels of Jane Austen are not merely *in* English; they *are* English. With its manors and balls and conventions of courtship and marriage, the British society portrayed in Austen's oeuvre is practically a character unto itself. And for a long time that national character, which propels so many of her heroines into their tribulations, was trickier to translate than the author's words. The first translations that appeared—some even before Austen's death—changed details freely to suit the tastes or knowledge of a foreign readership.

All six novels were published in French between 1815 and 1824. The editors of these *Bibliothèque britannique* editions, the brothers Marc-Auguste Pictet and Charles Pictet de Rochement, cared more about the opportunity to educate young Francophone ladies on the importance of decorum and less about preserving Austen's literary sensibilities. Poor Lizzy had many of her best bantering gems whittled down to demure responses. A later translation of *Raison et sensibilité* (*Sense and Sensibility*) by the Swiss novelist Isabelle de Montolieu likewise avowed "slight changes" that in fact changed the tone of the entire work.

Contemporary translations also cropped up in Germany, with similar cultural adjustments. The historical novelist and translator W. A. Lindau generally left the plots untouched but made sweeping stylistic alterations: Germanized names (including "Johanna Austen"), geographical references smoothed into general descriptions, and a neat excision of those English adverbs *particularly, especially, rather.* A later edition of *Stolz und Vorurtheil* (*Pride and Prejudice*) even changed the iconic first line, substituting "youth" and "wealth" for "possession" and "good fortune." Further muddying the waters, some translations were themselves based on translations: an 1836 Swedish *Familjen Elliot* (*Persuasion*) took for its source a French version titled *La Famille Elliot.*

Some cultural gulfs were simply too wide to cross. Though a review of *Emma* appeared in a Russian periodical in 1816, the first translation of Austen's work into Russian was published more than 150 years later, in 1967. Asian countries were also latecomers. The late-nineteenth-century Japanese literary set may have praised Austen, but the first edition of her work did not appear in Japan until 1926. Likewise, English-to-Chinese translation did not pick up until the turn of the twentieth century, although the translator Wei Yi had praised Austen's novels in his short 1917 book *Brief Profiles of Famous Western Novelists.*

These days, Austen has a worldwide following. There are Jane Austen Societies in North America, the United Kingdom, and Australia as well as in countries as far-flung as Brazil, Italy, Argentina, Spain, and the Netherlands. Fortunately, the art of translation has evolved, and translators now work carefully to respect and preserve source material. And like their English counterparts, the design of foreign-edition covers has changed with the times.

FRUNDSBERG-VIRLAG GMBH

This 1939 German edition of *Pride and Prejudice* changes the title, with Teutonic pragmatism, to what everyone cares about anyway—the relationship between the two main characters. The cover is fascinating in its way, with a rather detailed drawing of Elizabeth that looks as if it could be a copy of a late-eighteenth-century portrait. The stylized yet realistically rendered portrait is accompanied by a line-drawing silhouette of Mr. Darcy. The whole oozes thirties glamour despite the male figure's scrupulously period-correct attire.

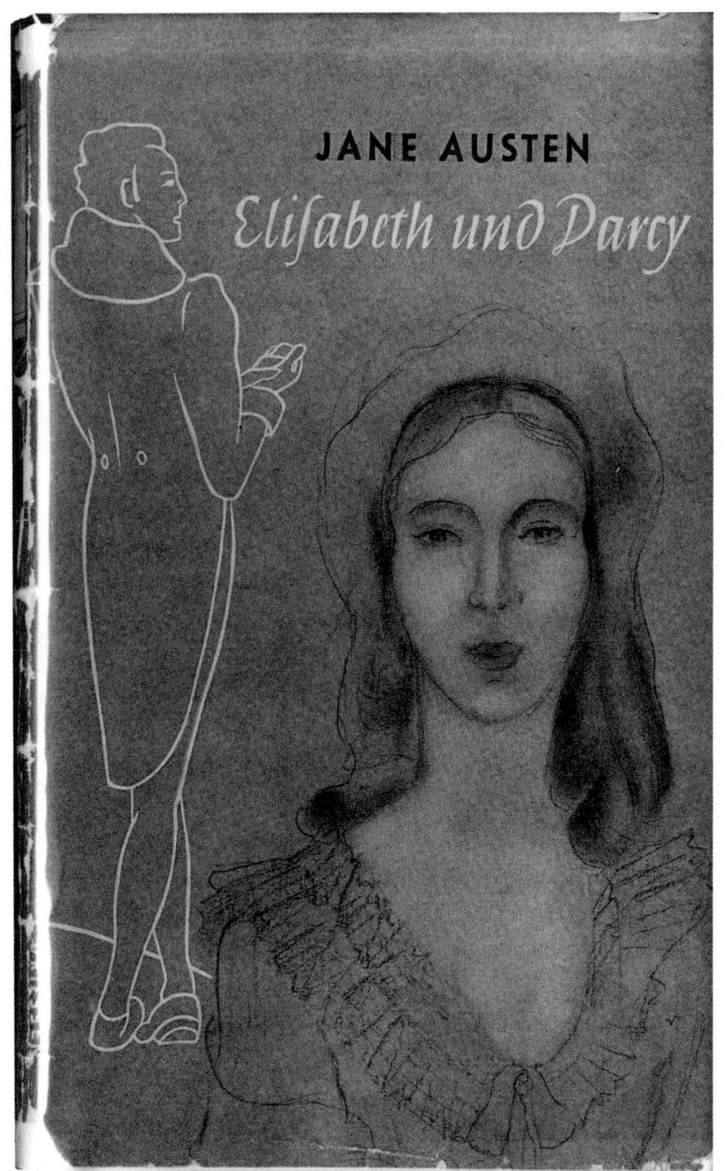

ITER EDICIONES S.A.

This 1970 Spanish student edition of *Pride and Prejudice* brings together the sleepy-eyed illustrative style of the late sixties and what appears to be the iconic black bowler hat of midcentury painter René Magritte. Whether the mini homage was intentional, the effect is inarguably surreal (and anachronistic—the bowler hat wasn't invented until 1849, much too late to top off one of Austen's heroes).

"You are charmingly group'd, and appear to uncommon advantage. The picturesque would be spoilt by admitting a fourth."

M. ARIMANY

Austen's works were translated into French, German, Swedish, and Danish in the nineteenth century, but Spanish translations did not appear until the early twentieth, with translations in the Castilian dialect (as spoken in Spain) distributed in Latin America. This Spanish edition of *Northanger Abbey*—titled *La Abadia de Northanger*—was published in Barcelona in 1945. It shows a vaguely period illustration of a ball, perhaps meant to be those at Bath attended by Catherine Morland and Henry Tilney, though Catherine would never be so alarmed by Henry as she appears to be here.

The cover image wraps around to the back, creating an attractive visual package.

EDITORIAL MIGUEL ARIMANY S.A.

A romantic pair graces the front cover of *En el Parque Mansfield*, a Spanish edition from 1954. Who is that pouty-lipped lady clenched in a rakish-looking gentleman's manly embrace? Surely not upright Fanny Price. Perhaps it's Maria Bertram and Henry Crawford, practicing her scenes from the play "Lover's Vows" (which involved embracing, which is why it was so shocking for them to practice those scenes, which is why they wanted to practice them so often).

Another attractive "wrap," this one featuring an evocative wash drawing in moody blue tones.

EDITRICE BOSCHI

What a gorgeous piece of fifties Italian style! On the smashing cover of this 1957 translation of *Pride and Prejudice*, it looks as if Jane Bennet is ready to zip over to Netherfield on her Vespa rather than riding on horseback. (Yet more impressive is that she managed such a coiffure before the invention of hairspray.)

ART: MUSATI; DESIGN: B. MIGLIARINI

"What made you so shy of me, when you first called, and afterwards dined here? Why, especially, when you called, did you look as if you did not care about me?"

—Pride and Prejudice

EDIZIONI SAS

Miss Woodhouse has descended from a Hollywood production of Rebecca of Sunnybrook Farm and onto the cover of this 1956 Italian translation. As with contemporary English editions, the styling of the cover model says much more about the ruby-lipped, straw-bonneted standards of mid-twentieth-century beauty than it does about period accuracy. Likewise, the poster-letter typography of the title would seem more at home in a 1950s movie house than a Regency parlor.

EDIZIONI SAS

The cover of this 1956 Italian translation of *Pride and Prejudice* is a photograph of the infamous archery scene from the 1940 Hollywood film adaptation (page 172). The scene does not occur in the novel, but it is certainly fine symbolism of the, shall we say, pointed relationship between Elizabeth and Mr. Darcy.

EDIZIONI CAPITOL

This 1961 Italian edition displays one of the issues that many readers have with some midcentury translations: the names of the characters are changed to make them sound more local. (At least Signorina Morland's given name was not changed to Caterina, and she does make a fine Italian beauty, albeit one who resembles Audrey Hepburn in *Roman Holiday*.) Modern foreign-language readers tend to prefer that the names be rendered as in the original.

DESIGN: STUDIO WISE

RCS LIBRI S.P.A.

The publishers of this 1998 Italian translation of *Northanger Abbey* expended minimal effort on design, instead concentrating on the text, which Italian Janeites have declared to be an excellent translation. As a modern edition, the original character names—Catherine, Henry, Eleanor, and so on—have properly been preserved.

No one who had ever seen Catherine Morland in her infancy would have supposed her born to be an heroine. Her situation in life, the character of her father and mother, her own person and disposition, were all equally against her.

COLLECTION L'EVENTAIL

The title here translates not to *Sense and Sensibility* but (loosely) *Heart and Reason*. The delightful alliteration of Austen's title was probably lost in translation anyway, and this cover illustration of Willoughby carrying Marianne back to Barton Cottage after she sprained her ankle is full of charm.

She had raised herself from the ground, but her foot had been twisted in her fall, and she was scarcely able to stand. The gentleman offered his services; and perceiving that her modesty declined what her situation rendered necessary, took her up in his arms without farther delay, and carried her down the hill.

WERNER SODERSTROM

The cover illustration of this 1951 Finnish edition follows the general trend by English-language publishers of depicting a scene from the novel. It shows Captain Wentworth glowering over his shoulder at Anne Elliot: "The evening ended with dancing. On its being proposed, Anne offered her services, as usual; and though her eyes would sometimes fill with tears as she sat at the instrument, she was extremely glad to be employed, and desired nothing in return but to be unobserved." The watercolor illustration is also typical for books at the time (just look at that cupid's-bow mouth).

AST

Forget love: *Mr. Darcy's wet shirt* is the universal language. This lovely cover illustration of a 2011 Russian translation of *Pride and Prejudice* is clearly reminiscent of Colin Firth and Jennifer Ehle in the 1995 miniseries adaptation (though this Darcy's hair is way pouffier). The inscription in the wax seal translates to "the beloved novel," which I believe Janeites worldwide can agree on (even if it was written by "Dzhein Ostin").

M. NEWMAN, INC.

The title for this 1952 Hebrew edition literally translates as *Love and Pride*, and although it loses the alliteration of the English original, it does have a nice rhyme to it in that language (*Ahava Ve'ga'avah*). However, the Hebrew word for "pride" does carry connotations of haughtiness . . . perhaps not unjustly for Mr. Darcy's attitude at the story's outset. The airy illustration presumably features the scene in which Darcy first confronts Wickham.

Mr. Wickham, after a few moments, touched his hat—a salutation which Mr. Darcy just deigned to return. What could be the meaning of it?—It was impossible to imagine; it was impossible not to long to know.

The ladies declared he was much handsomer than Mr. Bingley, and he was looked at with great admiration for about half the evening, till his manners gave a disgust which turned the tide of his popularity; for he was discovered to be proud, to be above his company, and above being pleased.

CHANGJIANG LITERATURE PRESS

The most interesting thing about this 2010 Chinese translation of *Pride and Prejudice* is not the generic cover illustration (a detail from the 1907 painting *In Love* by Marcus Stone) but the slimness of the volume. The book is the trim size as a normal trade paperback but runs only 173 pages—about the same thickness as the severely reduced and rewritten editions of the novels meant for middle-grade readers (see page 153). Presumably the character-based Chinese language reduced the amount of pages needed, but the translator may also have pruned the original text or it may have been otherwise shortened (that is, censored). The words at the bottom translate to "classic world literature collection, youth edition."

ART: MARCUS STONE, DETAIL FROM "IN LOVE"

MINEUMSA

This 2006 Korean translation of *Sense and Sensibility* uses the same portrait illustration as on the current Penguin Classics edition (page 183)—a detail from *Portrait of Ellen and Mary McIlvaine* by Thomas Sully. The 1834 painting is a little late for Austen's period, but the display of sisterly love works well for the novel, signaling to Korean readers that they should expect a translation of a British novel.

ART: THOMAS SULLY, DETAIL FROM "PORTRAIT OF ELLEN AND MARY MCILVAINE"

CHUKO BUNKO

The cover of this 1999 Japanese translation features *katakana* characters, the writing system used most for foreign words. Miss Woodhouse's name is particularly well suited: only two characters are needed ("E-Ma"). Jane Austen's name appears below the title, and the name of the Japanese translator is set within a scroll at the bottom. The charming, delicate illustration pairs Austen's matchmaker with a cupidinous companion.

SHINCHOSHA

This Japanese translation of *Pride and Prejudice* from 2010 takes a different tack with its cover, using an illustration that evokes both the time and place of the original and the culture of its target market. The image of a lady with her hair in a neat bun, showing a bit of decolletage as a Regency lady might, is reminiscent of Austen's period but speaks equally well to Japanese styles, with its echoes of *bijin-ga* ("beautiful person picture," portraits of Japanese women usually made as woodblock prints). The title is a translation, rather than a transliteration, and so is written in *kanji* (a system wherein each character represents an entire word, rather than a syllable). Of the many possible renderings of the word "pride," the translator here chose one with a positive connotation (good news for Team Darcy!).

AUSTENIANA

In the early part of the twentieth century, a Wisconsin native and Janeite named Alberta Hirschheimer attended Goucher College, in Baltimore. While there she met and, in 1930, married Henry Burke, a lawyer. Alberta brought to the marriage a shelf of Jane Austen novels as well as a copy of Geoffrey Keynes's *Jane Austen: A Bibliography*. Unlike most of Austen's heroines, Alberta Burke had inherited a fortune from her grandfather, and she was able to acquire rare books and other items related to Austen, her work, and her time. A few years after the marriage, a trip to England and the antiquarian bookstore Marks and Company set the Burkes on their path to becoming perhaps the most famous collectors of Austeniana in Janeite history.

First editions were easier to obtain in those days, and more cheaply—in 1937 Alberta paid 15 pounds 8 shillings for one of *Pride and Prejudice* and even less for Austen's other novels (such books now command in the five figures). The Burkes also formed relationships with auction houses and antiquarian dealers, who would let them know when interesting Austen-related items became available. Mrs. Burke acquired her first Austen-written letters in 1938. Her husband did much of the letter-writing and legwork, jokingly comparing his contribution to *Mansfield Park*'s busybody Mrs. Norris.

In 1935, Mrs. Burke began keeping notebooks in which she pasted every reference, no matter how small, to Jane Austen that she found in her extensive reading of newspapers and magazines, including three notebooks dedicated mostly to three adaptations of *Pride and Prejudice*. In the 1940s, the Burkes began collecting translations of Austen's work, facilitated both by their own travels and by friends who brought them books from foreign countries. One of their most exciting acquisitions was in 1948, when Alberta was able to purchase a lock of Jane Austen's hair (as well as a lock of Austen's father's hair) from Sotheby's. That summer, the Burkes attended the yearly meeting of the Jane Austen Society at Chawton, where Edward Carpenter, whose purchase of Chawton Cottage spurred the founding of the society, complained that the hair had been purchased by an American and would be taken out of the country. Decades later, Henry Burke described his wife's reaction: "Alberta muttered under her breath, 'I will give them the damn hair.' She then rose and said very simply, 'I am the American who bought Jane's hair and if the society would like to have it I shall be glad to make a contribution of the hair.' At that point, the tent in which the meeting was being held almost collapsed." The lock of hair is part of the permanent exhibit at Jane Austen's House Museum at Chawton Cottage.

The Burkes' collection included books not only related to Austen—first and other rare editions, translations, and works of criticism—but also about the culture of the late eighteenth and early nineteenth centuries, Austen's letters, original illustrations of the novels, and other ephemera. At Alberta Burke's death in 1975, much of her collection was bequeathed to Goucher College's Julia Rogers Library as the Alberta and Henry Burke Collection; the letters and other items went to the Morgan Library in New York. Four years later, Alberta's husband, Henry, cofounded the Jane Austen Society of North America.

Alberta Burke's collection is constantly in demand by students, scholars, and Janeites, and her notebooks have been scanned and made available on the Internet for the pleasure of fans worldwide. No doubt she would have been delighted with her legacy.

COLLECTING JANE

"And books!—Thomson, Cowper, Scott—she would buy them all over and over again: she would buy up every copy, I believe, to prevent their falling into unworthy hands; and she would have every book that tells her how to admire an old twisted tree."

—EDWARD FERRARS teasing Marianne Dashwood, *Sense and Sensibility*

If you've bought this book (or been given it as a gift), it's likely that you identify yourself as a book person. Perhaps you already collect books, but after seeing some of the beautiful, odd, artistic, intriguing editions reproduced on these pages, you now find yourself searching with a purpose: to amass a selection of Austen's works. Caring for your collection takes common sense and a bit of specialized knowledge. Here are some suggestions to set you on your acquisitive path.

Think like a librarian. Decide where to place the bookshelf that will hold your beloved books. Out of direct sunlight is best, and preferably in a low-humidity, well-ventilated area—dust and bugs are the death of books. Set aside a shelf or two at first, and plan to run out of space. Next, figure out a system—will the books be organized alphabetically by author or title, or chronological by publication date? You may want to take more of a design approach, setting a few of the more attractive covers to face out or adding other items of Austeniana to the display. Not only will you be able to admire them, but they will also contribute a literary element to your interior decor (this is often referred to, somewhat snarkily nowadays, as "styling").

Set 'em straight. You'll want to use bookends to keep books upright and firmly snug one next to the other so that the covers and pages don't warp (and pests have a harder time getting in). It's best to lay large and fragile or damaged books flat. If you have a particularly rare edition, consider storing it in an acid-free box and using a cradle or wedge when opening it. These and other archival materials for book and manuscript storage are easily found on the Web and in major craft stores and photography supply shops.

Keep your focus (and your budget). Jane Austen would disapprove of any imprudence, so be sure to buy within your means. Stop in regularly to bookshops and online marketplaces selling used editions (e.g., Advanced Book Exchange, Jane Austen Books, Etsy); be sure to set up e-mail alerts on eBay. Make friends with specialty booksellers, either virtually or personally—they are often happy to watch out for volumes of interest to their customers.

Enjoy it! This is perhaps the most important advice about assembling a collection. Show it off, either in your home or on the Internet. Fans will find you, and you'll build a network of friends to share and collect with.

He and I should not in the least agree, of course, in our ideas of novels and heroines. Pictures of perfection, as you know, make me sick and wicked.

—JANE AUSTEN, speaking of an acquaintance, to her niece Fanny Knight in a letter dated March 23, 1817

Jane Austen had strong ideas about her heroines, even going so far as to defend them and the art of novel writing in Chapter 5 of *Northanger Abbey*. Her characters are beloved, indeed, for all their faults as well as for their refinements, just as is her profession. So now, for those readers who need a quick refresher on the authoress's literary works, here are short summaries of her novels, juvenilia, and unpublished stories: "In short, only some work in which the greatest powers of the mind are displayed, in which the most thorough knowledge of human nature, the happiest delineation of its varieties, the liveliest effusions of wit and humour, are conveyed to the world in the best-chosen language."

JANE AUSTEN'S NOVELS

Sense and Sensibility

Working Title: *Elinor and Marianne*
Written: 1795
Revised: 1797 and 1809–10
Published: 1811

See pages 12, 14, 25, 28, 43, 55, 69, 80, 91, 94, 98, 103, 109, 112, 117, 119, 120, 130, 131, 136, 139, 147, 148, 150, 154, 157, 159, 183, 198, and 204.

Sense and Sensibility presents the stark realities of romance in Jane Austen's time. The complex story is softened with sometimes savage humor and a cast of memorable characters.

When their father dies, the Dashwood sisters—sensible Elinor and headstrong, romantic Marianne—are left without much in the way of fortune. Elinor's lover, Edward Ferrars, is secretly engaged to the vulgar, grasping Lucy Steele, who triumphs over Elinor while not allowing her to reveal the secret. Marianne has fallen in love with the dashing Willoughby. Colonel Brandon, the friend of a neighbor and nearly twenty years older than Marianne, admires her but understands that he doesn't stand a chance.

When Marianne learns that Willoughby is engaged to a rich young lady and will marry her within a few weeks, she is devastated and succumbs to her emotions. Her health suffers, and Elinor nurses her while nursing her own heartbreak over Edward; Marianne falls into a decline and nearly dies.

When the secret of Edward's engagement is revealed, his mother disinherits him, ironically freeing him from family constraints that prevent his marriage; fortunately for him, Lucy Steele fixes upon his now-rich younger brother, and Edward and Elinor are free to marry. Marianne recovers her health and learns that fiery passion can flame out, and that steady affection from a true heart, such as Colonel Brandon's, can be equally acceptable even to a romantic.

Pride and Prejudice

Working Title: *First Impressions*
Written: 1796–97
Revised: 1811–12
Published: 1813

See pages 13, 24, 25, 26, 32, 36, 39, 40, 42, 48, 50, 51, 56, 59, 64, 65, 75, 79, 80, 87, 90, 95, 96, 100, 103, 104, 106, 107, 108, 115, 118, 120, 122, 124, 125, 132, 135, 137, 146, 150, 151, 152, 155, 156, 158, 159, 160, 172, 173, 174, 182, 188, 189, 192, 195, 200, 203, and 206.

One of the most famous opening lines in literature, "It is a truth universally acknowledged that a single man in possession of a good fortune must be in want of a wife," gets Jane Austen's best-known work off to a rousing start. The heroine, Elizabeth Bennet, is one of five sisters; her father's estate is entailed on a distant cousin, and her silly, shallow mother is anxious to get the girls married off, a difficult task in the face of their limited fortunes. Mrs. Bennet is delighted when a rich young man, Mr. Bingley, leases a nearby estate, hoping that one of her daughters will take his fancy. Mr. Bingley obliges her by taking an obvious interest in the beautiful eldest daughter, Jane. He has an even richer friend, Mr. Darcy, staying with him, but Mr. Darcy's arrogant pride disgusts the neighborhood in general and Elizabeth in particular. Nonetheless, Mr. Darcy shows a marked interest in Elizabeth, though he is often the victim of her lively wit.

A series of misunderstandings, marriage proposals, and elopements ensues, with Elizabeth and Mr. Darcy learning to better understand themselves and each other. They become engaged at the end of the book, and the attentive reader knows that it is more than a match between a rich man and a pretty girl: it is a true meeting of minds, hearts, and two complex, complementary personalities.

Mansfield Park

Written: 1812–13
Published: 1814

See pages 15, 25, 49, 52, 53, 70, 84, 88, 89, 103, 105, 113, 114, 137, 181, 191, and 201.

The heroine of *Mansfield Park*, Fanny Price, is a humble relation brought up at the titular estate of her wealthy uncle, Sir Thomas Bertram. Fanny's cousin Edmund Bertram, destined for the church, is kind to her and directs her reading and education, while her aunts make her a sort of unpaid servant who fetches and carries and acts as a companion.

The social world of the Park is turned upside down with the arrival of Mary and Henry Crawford, the sister and brother of the rector's wife. The Bertram sisters are interested in Henry, and he is in return interested in the eldest daughter, Maria, who is already engaged to a stupid but rich man. Edmund is attracted to Mary Crawford and confides in Fanny. Fanny is in love with Edmund, and these revelations, and Edmund's rationalization of Mary's moral shortcomings, distress her. Fanny suffers even more when Henry Crawford, having toyed with her cousins' hearts, turns his attention to her. Henry falls in love with Fanny and proposes; Fanny, having witnessed his cruel behavior to her cousins, cannot accept him. Sir Thomas, not understanding Fanny's reticence in the face of such an excellent potential marriage, sends her back to her own family in Portsmouth. The Prices are relatively poor, but Fanny perseveres and her refusal of Henry Crawford is shown to be right when he has an affair with the now-married Maria. Fanny is welcomed back to Mansfield Park and eventually into Edmund's heart as well.

Emma

Written: 1814–15

Published: 1815

See pages 16, 17, 25, 29, 44, 45, 60, 66, 82, 91, 92, 101, 103, 109, 119, 120, 126, 127, 138, 142, 143, 144, 145, 175, 176, 177, 184, 194, and 205.

Emma Woodhouse, "handsome, clever, and rich," and only twenty-one years old, is the social queen of Highbury. Everyone defers to her—everyone, that is, except her neighbor, Mr. Knightley, the only person who ever criticizes Emma's behavior.

Convinced that her own endeavors brought about a marriage between her former governess and a neighbor, Emma sets out to make another match between the vicar, Mr. Elton, and a young lady of obscure background, Harriet Smith. She learns, to her dismay, that Mr. Elton actually is interested in Emma herself (or in her fortune of thirty thousand pounds). Mr. Elton marries a vulgar social climber from Bristol, who takes an interest in Jane Fairfax, the orphaned granddaughter of the late vicar. Jane has no fortune, but was educated to become a governess, and Mrs. Elton sets out to find her a proper situation.

Mrs. Weston's stepson, Frank Churchill, comes to Highbury, and Emma is interested in him at first but then decides to make a match between Frank and Harriet. Unfortunately for Emma, Harriet has other ideas, revealing that she prefers Mr. Knightley. Emma realizes that Harriet cannot marry Mr. Knightley—indeed, no one can, except Emma herself. Things are sorted out amicably, and the happy couple has only the obstacle of Emma's valetudinarian father to overcome.

Northanger Abbey

Working Title: *Susan*

Written: 1798–1803

Revised: 1816

Published: 1818

See pages 18, 25, 31, 54, 57, 58, 62, 64, 66, 67, 68, 74, 78, 83, 84, 88, 103, 116, 128, 138, 149, 190, 196, and 197.

Composed when Jane Austen was in her early twenties, *Northanger Abbey* is a bridge between the rollicking humor of the stories Jane wrote as a young girl and her more mature work. It is an affectionately comic parody of the Gothic and sentimental novels popular in her time as well as a coming-of-age story of the naive but lovable heroine, Catherine Morland. Catherine is not a typical heroine: she is not a prodigy, nor is she accomplished, well-read, or even beautiful, though she can manage "almost pretty" on a good day. Invited to Bath by rich, childless neighbors, she meets Henry Tilney, a young clergyman who amuses her with witty nonsense, and Isabella Thorpe, a fashionable young lady who introduces her to the delights of "horrid" Gothic novels such as Ann Radcliffe's *Mysteries of Udolpho*.

Isabella's brother John attempts to court Catherine, but she thinks him crude and vulgar and remains interested in Henry Tilney. Catherine's brother James becomes engaged to Isabella, but Isabella distresses Catherine by flirting with Henry's elder brother, the heir of Northanger Abbey. Henry's father, General Tilney, takes an interest in Catherine, and Henry's sister, Eleanor, invites her to the Abbey. There, Catherine's imagination, inspired by horrid novels, takes a morbid turn, and she begins to imagine strange things about the General; Henry disabuses her of these notions, but later, the General shows himself to be little better than the villain that she had imagined. Catherine learns to trust her instincts; namely, that people do not always mean what they say; that real life is not like books, especially of the horrid variety; that a hero can be quite an ordinary fellow; and that villains can be quite dastardly even without committing murder.

Persuasion

Written: 1816

Published: 1818

See pages 18, 25, 37, 46, 55, 56, 62, 81, 85, 91, 93, 94, 97, 99, 102, 113, 116, 120, 128, 138, 140, 147, 180, and 199.

Jane Austen's final completed novel is a story of second chances. In the summer of 1806, Anne Elliot became engaged to Frederick Wentworth, a newly promoted naval officer waiting for a ship of his own. Under pressure from snobbish relatives who consider a half-pay officer not good enough for a baronet's daughter, and herself convinced that a wife will hold Wentworth back in his career, Anne reluctantly breaks off the engagement.

Eight years later, circumstances have changed: Anne's father, a "foolish, spendthrift baronet," is so much in debt that he must let the family estate and move to Bath. The house is leased by an admiral, coincidentally married to Captain Wentworth's sister, and Wentworth, who has made a fortune in the war and is still angry over the broken engagement, arrives for a visit. Anne, her own youthful bloom lost from eight years of unhappiness and regret, must watch while he flirts with two pretty young girls. A tragic event brings them together for a short time, but she leaves for Bath thinking he is lost to her forever, until circumstances change and love gets a second chance.

OTHER WORKS BY JANE AUSTEN

Many of these works were not published until the twentieth century, most as part of the Oxford Illustrated Editions edited by R. W. Chapman.

The "Juvenilia"

Three notebooks into which Jane copied stories that she wrote when she was a young girl. Works include, among others:

The Beautifull Cassandra

A short but precociously over-the-top tale parodying the sentimental fiction of the late eighteenth century in which we follow the "beautifull" title character through a day's unusually violent adventures.

See page 76.

Catharine, or the Bower

Catharine, a young woman just entering society, is an orphan who lives with her aunt in the country. She creates a bower on the property to which she retreats when upset or unhappy. Catharine goes to a ball, makes friends with the young ladies of the neighborhood, and embarks on a romance with a neighbor's son; the nascent story starts off much like several of Austen's mature novels, but without the acquired skill of the later work.

See pages 79 and 86.

Love and Freindship

This is another hilarious parody of sentimental fiction, written as a series of letters from the main character, Laura, to her friend's daughter, Marianne. Laura experiences all the fortunes and misfortunes a heroine can: elopement, cruel relatives, unknown relatives, sudden fortune, even more sudden death, and (with a friend) fainting "alternately onto a sofa." The misspelling "freindship" occurs in Austen's original manuscript.

History of England

"By a Partial, Prejudiced, and Ignorant Historian." A parody of serious histories, this short work gives brief, humorous overviews of the reign of each British monarch from Henry IV through Charles I. Cassandra Austen added illustrations of the various kings and queens. The manuscript is in the possession of the British Library and facsimile editions with the illustrations are widely available.

See page 77.

WORKS UNPUBLISHED IN AUSTEN'S LIFETIME

Lady Susan

A novella in letters; the title character is an amoral, manipulative sociopath who uses others indiscriminately, somewhat reminiscent of Madame de Merteuil of *Les Liaisons Dangereuses*. Jane Austen never attempted to publish it, but technically it is brilliantly executed. It was first published in the second edition of J. E. Austen-Leigh's *Memoir of Jane Austen*.

See page 78.

The Watsons

A rather darker version of *Pride and Prejudice*, this incomplete work sets up the story of the Watson sisters, three of whom are trying very hard to get married, as they have no mother and a sickly clergyman father who will leave them with nothing when he dies.

See pages 38 and 78.

Sanditon

Jane Austen worked on this novel until a few months before her death, completing twelve chapters. The heroine, Charlotte Heywood, is invited to a small seaside town called Sanditon and meets the Parker family: the eldest Mr. Parker, who is promoting the town as a resort destination; his two sisters, Susan and Diana, and youngest brother, Arthur, all determined hypochondriacs; and his younger brother Sidney, who seems destined to be the hero of the piece. Brilliantly ironic and savagely funny, *Sanditon* might have been Jane Austen's finest novel had she lived to finish it.

See pages 78 and 110.

Bibliography

"Alberta Burke's Notebooks." Notebook no. 1, Letter 10. http://meyerhoff.goucher.edu/library/Web_folder_Jane_Austen_Books/Composition_book_1/cb1110.htm

Amano, Miyuki, Hiroshi Ebine, and Kazuko Hisamori. "Jane Austen in Japanese Literature: An Overview." *Persuasions On-Line* 30, no. 2 (2010). http://www.jasna.org/persuasions/on-line/vol30no2/introduction.html

Baines, Phil. *Penguin by Design*. New York: Penguin, 2005.

Cossy, Valérie, and Diego Saglia. "Translations." *Jane Austen in Context*. Ed. Janet Todd. Cambridge, Eng.: Cambridge University Press, 2005, 169–181.

Eliot, Simon. "The business of Victorian publishing." *The Cambridge Companion to the Victorian Novel*. Ed. Deirdre David. Cambridge and New York: The Cambridge University Press (2001)

Fergus, Jan. *Jane Austen: A Literary Life*. London: Macmillan, 1991.

———. "Biography." *Jane Austen in Context*. Ed. Janet Todd. Cambridge, Eng.: Cambridge University Press, 2005.

———. "The Literary Marketplace." *A Companion to Jane Austen*. Ed. Claudia L. Johnson and Clara Tuite. Malden, Mass.: Wiley-Blackwell, 2012.

———. "The Professional Woman Writer." *The Cambridge Companion to Jane Austen*. Ed. Edward Copeland and Juliet McMaster. Cambridge, Eng.: Cambridge University Press, 1997, 12–31.

García Soria, Cinthia. "Austen Illustrators Henry and Charles Brock." Mollands.net, http://www.mollands.net/etexts/other/brocks.html

Gilson, David. *A Bibliography of Jane Austen*. New Castle, Del.: Oak Knoll Press, 1977.

———. "Later Publishing History, with Illustrations." *Jane Austen in Context*. Ed. Janet Todd. Cambridge, Eng.: Cambridge University Press, 2005.

Halsey, Katie. *Jane Austen and Her Readers, 1786–1945*. London and New York: Anthem Press, 2013.

Howe, Mark, and Antony DeWolfe. "A Jane Austen Letter with Other 'Janeana' from an Old Book of Autographs," *Yale Review* 15 (1925/1926): 319–335.

Johnson, Claudia L. "Austen Cults and Cultures." *The Cambridge Companion to Jane Austen*. Ed. Edward Copeland and Juliet McMaster. Cambridge, Eng.: Cambridge University Press, 1997, 211–226.

Kaplan, Laurie, and Nancy Magnuson. *Twenty-Five Years of Jane Austen*. Goucher College, 2000.

Leurs, Laurens. "The History of Print from 1800 to 1899." PrePressure.com, http://www.prepressure.com/printing/history/1800-1899

———. "The History of Print from 1900 to 1999." PrePressure.com, http://www.prepressure.com/printing/history/1900-1999

Raven, James. "Book production." *Jane Austen in Context*. Ed. Janet Todd. Cambridge, Eng.: Cambridge University Press, 2005.

Southam, Brian. "Texts and Editions." *A Companion to Jane Austen*. Ed. Claudia L. Johnson and Clara Tuite. Malden, Massachusetts: Wiley-Blackwell, 2012.

Sutherland, Kathryn. *Jane Austen's Textual Lives: from Aeschylus to Bollywood*. New York: Oxford University Press, 2005.

Yaffe, Deborah. *Among the Janeites*. Boston: Mariner Books, 2013.

Acknowledgments

There are no two ways about it: I had a lot of help with this book. Friends and family and acquaintances came through with books and scans: Heather Laurence, stalwart of Team Tilney and keeper of the Inadvertently Gothic and Completely Unabridged *Northanger Abbey*s; Laurel Ann Nattress for plumbing her wonderful collection, as well as pointing me toward some interesting items I had forgotten or never knew about; Laura Boyle, whose enthusiasm, friendship, creativity, and support never flag; Rita Kirkwood (my Number One Fan), Dennis Kirkwood, Jerry Sullivan, and Megan Kirkwood Horan, for lending and scannage and love; Linda Troost, who doesn't even know me and yet good-naturedly scanned the cover of her vintage Penguin *Persuasion* (seriously, Janeites are the *best*); Tara Olivero at Goucher College Library for turning me loose in the special collections room one memorable day; Cinthia García Soria for assistance with information about Spanish translations of Austen, and for links to all those eBay auctions of Brock-illustrated editions; and Allison Thompson for sharing information about early French translations and for talking me off the ledge when I really needed it. Thanks to all at Quirk Books, especially Jason Rekulak, for giving me this great and fun opportunity, and Blair Thornburgh for her Fanny Price–like patience (not to mention sorting out the manuscript and scans like Fanny did Lady Bertram's needlework). Much love to the Horatians and Janeites from all over the world whose friendship and support never cease to amaze and humble me. Thanks to the readers of AustenBlog who have provided so much fun and information over the years. Thanks to Jane Austen, of course, without whose work (specifically, Captain Wentworth's letter to Anne Elliot *oh my godfathers the goosebumps*) this book would not have been possible. And thanks to you, Gentle Reader, who makes it all worthwhile. I hope this journey through two hundred years of Austen has been as enjoyable for you as it has been for me.

A Note from the Author

Sometimes the most insignificant things lead to the most unexpected and glorious places. As with Mr. Darcy's love for Elizabeth Bennet, "I cannot fix on the hour" more precisely than to say sometime in the early 1990s, when I found myself in a mall drugstore, facing the mass market paperbacks rack, looking for something to read. Nothing appealed until a paperback caught my eye—an image of a smiling lady in a white gown and a big green bonnet. It was *Emma* by Jane Austen. I had recently been reading and rereading Victorian novels, particularly those by the Brontë sisters, and was drawn to this book by the pretty painting. People had been telling me for years that I should read Jane Austen, and the decision was made. The sticker on the cover for $2—the book was marked down for clearance—might have been persuasive as well.

I took the book home and read it, and I liked it. A little while later, I was in another bookstore and purchased a copy of *Pride and Prejudice*, which I also liked. A little while after that, I was in yet another bookstore and purchased a copy of *Persuasion*, and then I fell in love. I read Austen's three other novels, biographies of her life, and works of criticism. Soon came the mid-1990s spate of Austen film adaptations to feed my new obsession. I started writing about Austen on the Internet. I joined the Jane Austen Society of North America. I started a blog. I wrote some books.

These things were all a direct consequence of my purchase of that two-dollar paperback. I can say with confidence that it changed my life. Jane Austen is powerful, and she can do that; she has done it for others besides me. Thank you, Jane, for everything.

ART: DAIRD, "MADAME DE SERISIAT COL FIGLIO"

Short and easy will be the task of the mere biographer. A life of usefulness, literature, and religion, was not by any means a life of event.

—Henry Austen, "Biographical Notice of the Author" published with *Northanger Abbey* and *Persuasion*, 1817